"*Your Religion Lived Out Loud*"

"PUTTING THE WORD OF GOD IN ACTION!"

CALVIN L. MCCULLOUGH SR.

WESTBOW
PRESS®
A DIVISION OF THOMAS NELSON
& ZONDERVAN

WestBow Press books may be ordered through booksellers or by contacting:

WestBow Press
A Division of Thomas Nelson & Zondervan
1663 Liberty Drive
Bloomington, IN 47403
www.westbowpress.com
844-714-3454

ISBN: 978-1-6642-4574-7 (sc)
ISBN: 978-1-6642-4575-4 (hc)
ISBN: 978-1-6642-4573-0 (e)

Library of Congress Control Number: 2021919785

Print information available on the last page.

WestBow Press rev. date: 10/25/2021

Contents

Foreword

Because it is our heart's desire that every man, woman, boy, and girl live a life that would bring glory to God, we would love for you to use this book in the same manner as Paul instructed Timothy to be the best person he could be. In this way, you could strengthen your spiritual growth.

There are a few questions all believers should ask themselves: What does a Christian truly look like? What type of words should come from a Christian mouth? And how should a Christian respond and function in a sinful world.

In First Timothy 4:12, the Apostle Paul tells Timothy and all Christians to "set an example for the believers." Paul points out to us how a true followers of Jesus Christ should look, sound and carry themselves as Christians.

Jesus uses two simple things (salt and light) in Matthew 5:13-16 to illustrate who we are and what we should be as His disciples. First salt: Salt creates a thirst, it is for seasons, it preserves, and salt maintains its character. Second, light: Light shines, it gives direction, and gives godly influence so others may see the good work and desire to discover what makes you different. Therefore, all Christians should be salt and light.

This book is a tool to help to us consciously walk in the truth of God's Word, bring Him glory and help us in our spiritual growth.

Dedication

Jesus, we thank you for your Love, your Mercy, your Peace and your Grace. We thank you for the blood you shed so we may share in your righteousness and gain a right relationship with God the Father through you.

"This Book is Dedicated to our Lord Jesus Christ the true teacher and the perfecter of our Holiness!"

Also, in Memory of my Fathers
Robert J. Wilmore and Lewis "Duke" Ingram

And the 2015 & 2016
South Pointe HS Football Team Bible Study Group

Introduction

First Timothy is a letter the Apostle Paul wrote to instruct a young man named Timothy. The Bible tells us that Paul of Tarsus was born with the name was Saul. In Philippians chapter three he called himself an Israelite of the tribe of Benjamin, a Hebrew of Hebrews; regarding the law, a Pharisee. As a Pharisee (which means "the separated ones" in Hebrew), Paul studied under the top rabbi (teacher) of his day, Gamaliel.

Saul was one of the leaders against the church of Jesus Christ. He persecuted the believers in Jerusalem, and he obtained permission from the Jewish leaders to go to other places to do the same. But on his way to Damascus he had an encounter with Jesus (Acts 9:1-19 NIV); Jesus revealed to him, that he was persecuting the God he was professing to serve by destroying the church. From this encounter, Saul became a believer in Jesus Christ; he changed his name to Paul when he began his evangelistic ministry.

Now the Bible tells us that Paul met Timothy in Lystra (modern day Turkey). Timothy was the child of a mixed marriage. His mother's name was Eunice and his grandmother was named Lois; they were Jewish and believers, but Timothy's father was a Greek (Acts 16:1 NIV).

Timothy's faith grew stronger and flourished so every Christian in the area "spoke well of him" (Acts 16:2 NIV).

Paul was impressed with Timothy and wanted to take him along with him on his mission trip, so Paul circumcised him because the Jews all knew that his father was a Greek. Afterwards the elders from his hometown lay hands on him to commission him for the ministry. Timothy worked with Paul and also represented him on at least three mission trips. Paul viewed Timothy as a son and not a co-worker. Paul called him "my son whom I love, who is faithful in the Lord" (1 Corinthians 4:17 NIV).

When Paul was arrested Jerusalem; Timothy went to the churches to encourage and strengthen them. During this time, Paul wrote First Timothy. Timothy was in Ephesus when Paul was writing him these instructions for the issues in the church and for his personal conduct as a Christian leader.

Our study comes from First Timothy 4:11-16 which states:

> Command and teach these things. Don't let anyone look down on you because you are young, but set an example for the believers in speech, in conduct, in love, in faith and in purity. Until I come, devote yourself to the public reading of Scripture, to preaching and to teaching. Do not neglect your gift, which was given you through prophecy when the body of elders laid their hands on you. Be diligent in these matters; give yourself wholly to them, so that everyone may see your progress. Watch your life and doctrine closely. Persevere in them, because if you do, you will save both yourself and your hearers (1 Timothy 4:11-16 NIV).

Instructions

We give all praises to our Lord and Savior Jesus because you are reading this book and have continued in your discipleship training. This means you or someone close to you has a true interest in your spiritual growth in Christ Jesus.

This program is for individual person study, one-on-one discipling, small groups, and/or Sunday School.

It is very important that you take time on each session; this means that some sessions will take more than one week. Take your time. You will be blessed and grow if you do the homework assignments and allow each person to discuss his or her assigned work.

We have also added Bible verses on each subject; so please take the time and discuss each verse in detail.

How to start:

Session 1: Overview of the Sessions

First: Open the Session with Prayer . . .
Second: Answer the Icebreaker question . . .
Third: Read 1 Timothy 4:11-16 (NIV)

Icebreaker Questions:

1. Has there ever been a time when you felt that people didn't take you seriously? Who, When and What?
2. Have you told anyone that you were serious about being a Christian? How did it make you feel? If you haven't told anyone, why not?
3. How does it feel, that people know that you are a Christian?

First Timothy 4:11-16 (NIV)

Command and teach these things. Don't let anyone look down on you because you are young, but set an example for the believers in speech, in conduct, in love, in faith and in purity. Until I come, devote yourself to the public reading of Scripture, to preaching and to teaching. Do not neglect your gift, which was given you through prophecy when the body of elders laid their hands on you.

Be diligent in these matters; give yourself wholly to them, so that everyone may see your progress. Watch your life and doctrine closely. Persevere in them, because if you do, you will save both yourself and your hearers.

List three things these verses are saying to you.

- _____
- _____
- _____

The Key Points to today's Scriptures Verses:

I. **Verse 11:** "Command and teach these things."

1. The first key point we find is a command: "command" means to order, tell, direct, or instruct.
2. Back in 1 Timothy 4:6 (NIV), Paul tells us: "If you point these things out to the brothers and sisters you will be a good minister of Christ Jesus, nourished on the truths of the faith and of the good teaching that you have followed."
3. The command is for all seasoned and mature Christians to teach the new or young Christian how to develop the character of Christ Jesus. What things . . . we find them in verse 12 (NIV).

II. **Verse 12:** "Don't let anyone look down on you because you are young,"

1. In The second command "Don't let anyone look down on you because you are young." Paul tells us not to let people look down on us because of our age, race, sex, economic situation, or our past sinful lives.
   a. Age: There is no age in which anyone becomes a perfect Christian (there is none).
   b. Race: Christianity has no color (It is not black, white, green, blue or any other color), shape or size! (Galatian 3:28 NIV).
   c. Sex: Christianity is not male or female (Galatian 3:28 NIV).
   d. Economic Situation: Salvation is a gift from God (Romans 5:16 NLT).
   e. Past sinful life, or "BC Days" (Before Christ Days): the key word is "Past." The Bible tells us, "Therefore if anyone is in Christ, he is a new creation. The old has passed away; behold, the new has come" (2 Corinthians 5:17 NIV).

2. Please understand, if someone is judging you because of one or more of these things, this book is the perfect study program for them.

III. In the third part of verse 12 is where we find the third command: "but set an example for the believers."

1. Timothy was to be an example in behavior. His conduct was to be an example of discipline, godliness, righteousness, and control. He was to demonstrate what a true follower and leader of the Jesus Christ looked like.
    *   "Be an example" in the Greek means: "become a pattern."

2. Paul also made this command to Titus, which states: "In all things show yourself to be an example of good deeds, with purity in doctrine, dignified, sound in speech which is beyond reproach, so that the opponent will be put to shame, having nothing bad to say about us" (Titus 2:7-8 NASB).

3. Below I have listed the ways in which Paul commands that Christians should act to be an example for the believers and for the unbelievers:
    *   in speech
    *   in conduct
    *   in love
    *   in faith
    *   in purity
    *   in the Word of God
    *   in being a good steward of your Gift
    *   and in doctrine

IV. Homework Assignment:

1. Remember the Eight (8) areas of a true Christian:
    *   Christian Speech
    *   Christian Conduct
    *   Christian Love
    *   Christian Faith
    *   Christian Purity
    *   The Word of God in the Christian life
    *   A good steward of my Christian Gift
    *   Christian Doctrine

Prayer: Father God, please help us to be doers of your Word, and not only hearers of your Word. Please help us grow in your Word and become closer to you. In Jesus' name – AMEN.

Session 2: "Speech"

First: Open the session with prayer . . .
Second: Check session 1 Homework assignment . . .

Icebreaker Questions:

1. Have you ever said something you wish you could take back? How did it make you feel?
2. Do you know of a person of whom you have never heard them say anything negative? Who is that person and how do you feel about that person?
3. What is the difference between Cursing and Profanity (cussing)?

Note: Profanity and Cursing

- Profanity (cussing) is abusive language that is offensive because it is disrespectful of religion or offensive because it is rude. Religious profanity is called blasphemy.
- Cursing is a solemn utterance intended to invoke a supernatural power to inflict harm or punishment on someone or something (telling someone to go to Hades or saying "I wish you would die").

Verse 12: "Don't let anyone look down on you because you are young, but set an example for the believers in *speech*, in conduct, in love, in faith and in purity" (1 Timothy 4:12 NIV).

I.   Verse 12: example for the believers: *"in speech"*

Here in verse 12 Paul tells Timothy to set an example for the believers in the way he talked in public and in private. He was to be an example in word: in what he said and in the way he said it. He had to control his conversation and tongue no matter the opposition.

In today's world, we hear it all – the good, the bad and the ugly. We hear it from adults, teenagers and little babies just learning to talk, cursing and using profanity. However, as a Christian you are

4

called to a higher standard. In the next section, we will see what the Word of God have to say about our *speech*.

II. What do the Bible haves to say about our *speech*? Take the time to discuss each verse.

1. "The tongue has the power of life and death, and those who love it will eat its fruit" (Proverbs 18:21 NIV).
   - What does Proverbs 18:21 speak to you? And how does it relate to your speech?

   - _____
   - _____
   - _____

2. "But I tell you that every careless word that people speak, they shall give an accounting for it in the day of judgment. "For by your words you will be justified, and by your words you will be condemned" (Matthew 12:36-37 NIV).
   - What does Matthew 12:36-37 say to you? And how does it relate to your speech?

   - _____
   - _____
   - _____

3. "Let your conversation be always full of grace, seasoned with salt, so that you may know how to answer everyone" (Colossians 4:6 NIV).
   - What does Colossians 4:6 say to you? And how does it relate to your speech?

   - _____
   - _____
   - _____

4. ". . . and soundness of speech that cannot be condemned, so that those who oppose you may be ashamed because they have nothing bad to say about us" (Titus 2:8 NIV).
   - What does Titus 2:8 say to you? And how does it relate to your speech?

- _____
- _____
- _____

5. "Pleasant words are as a honeycomb, sweet to the soul, and health to the bones" (Proverbs 16:24 KJV).
   - What does Proverbs 16:24 say to you? And how does it relate to your "Speech?"
   - _____
   - _____
   - _____

6. "The one who has knowledge uses words with restraint, and whoever has understanding is even-tempered" (Proverbs 17:27 NIV).
   - What does Proverbs 17:27 say to you? And how does it relate to your speech?
   - _____
   - _____
   - _____

7. "The words of a wise man's mouth are gracious; but the lips of a fool will swallow up himself" (Ecclesiastes 10:12 KJV).
   - What does Ecclesiastes 10:12 say to you? And how does it relate to your speech?
   - _____
   - _____
   - _____

8. "With the tongue we praise our Lord and Father, and with it we curse human beings, who have been made in God's likeness. Out of the same mouth come praise and cursing. My brothers and sisters, this should not be" (James 3:9-10 NIV).
   - What does James 3:9-10 say to you? And how does it relate to your speech?
   - _____
   - _____
   - _____

9. "Do not let any unwholesome talk come out of your mouths, but only what is helpful for building others up according to their needs, that it may benefit those who listen" (Ephesians 4:29 NIV).
   - What does Ephesians 4:29 say to you? And how does it relate to your speech?
   - _____
   - _____
   - _____

10. "But the things that come out of a person's mouth come from the heart, and these defile them" (Matthew 15:18 NIV).
    - What does Matthew 15:18 say to you? And how does it relate to your speech?
    - _____
    - _____
    - _____

11. "A good man brings good things out of the good stored up in his heart, and an evil man brings evil things out of the evil stored up in his heart. For the mouth speaks what the heart is full of" (Luke 6:45 NIV).
    - What does Luke 6:45 say to you? And how does it relate to your speech?
    - _____
    - _____
    - _____

12. "If you declare with your mouth, "Jesus is Lord," and believe in your heart that God raised him from the dead, you will be saved. For it is with your heart that you believe and are justified, and it is with your mouth that you profess your faith and are saved" (Romans 10:9-10 NIV).
    - What does Romans 10:9-10 say to you? And how does it relate to your speech?
    - _____
    - _____
    - _____

III. Homework Assignment:

1. **Speech** – ONLY say positive things.
2. This week's homework assignment is to use *speech* only for using positive and encouraging words with to everyone you encounter. Each day find one family member, one friend and one stranger and say something nice or encouraging.

    a. Day one:
   - Write in the person's name: _____
   - What did you say: _____
   - Write in the person name: _____
   - What did you say: _____
   - Write in the person name: _____
   - What did you say: _____

    b. Day two:
   - Write in the person's name: _____
   - What did you say: _____
   - Write in the person name: _____
   - What did you say: _____
   - Write in the person name: _____
   - What did you say: _____

    c. Day three:
   - Write in the person's name: _____
   - What did you say: _____
   - Write in the person name: _____
   - What did you say: _____
   - Write in the person name: _____
   - What did you say: _____

    d. Day four:
   - Write in the person's name: _____
   - What did you say: _____
   - Write in the person name: _____
   - What did you say: _____

- Write in the person name: _____
- What did you say: _____

e. Day five:
   - Write in the person's name: _____
   - What did you say: _____
   - Write in the person name: _____
   - What did you say: _____
   - Write in the person name: _____
   - What did you say: _____

f. Day six:
   - Write in the person's name: _____
   - What did you say: _____
   - Write in the person name: _____
   - What did you say: _____
   - Write in the person name: _____
   - What did you say: _____

g. Day seven:
   - Write in the person's name: _____
   - What did you say: _____
   - Write in the person name: _____
   - What did you say: _____
   - Write in the person name: _____
   - What did you say: _____

Prayer:
Lord God please put a guard over my mouth that nothing negative may come from my lips. Help me to speak only life, love and encouragement into the lives of others, In Jesus' Name – AMEN.

Session 3: "Conduct"

First: Open the session with prayer . . .
Second: Check session 2 Homework assignment . . .

Icebreaker Questions:

1. Tell of a time when you did not respond the right way?
2. Tell of a time when you saw a non-Christian responding like a non-Christian?
3. Tell of a time when you saw someone responding like a Christian?

Verse 12: Don't let anyone look down on you because you are young, but set an example for the believers in speech, in *conduct*, in love, in faith and in purity (1 Timothy 4:12 NIV).

I. Verse 12: example for the believers: "*Conduct*"

Like Timothy, every believer is called to the same high standards of conduct worthy of their honored position in Christ. True believers are to "walk the walk" and "talk the talk" with Christ like morals and behavior to the glory of God.

Integrity is not used much in today's English. One definition of integrity is: "the quality or state of being of sound moral principle; uprightness, honesty, and sincerity." So, we can say that a good synonym for integrity is honesty.

II. What does the Bible have to say about our *conduct*? Take the time to discuss each verse.

1. "Reject every kind of evil" / "Abstain from all appearance of evil" (1 Thessalonians 5:22 NIV).
   • What does 1 Thessalonians 5:22: say to you? And how does it relate to your conduct?
   • _____
   • _____
   • _____

2. "Whatever happens, conduct yourselves in a manner worthy of the gospel of Christ. Then, whether I come and see you or only hear about you in my absence, I will know that you stand firm in the one Spirit, striving together as one for the faith of the gospel" (Philippians 1:27 NIV).
   - What does Philippians 1:27 say to you? And how does it relate to your conduct?
     - _____
     - _____
     - _____

3. "So, in everything, do to others what you would have them do to you, for this sums up the Law and the Prophets" (Matthew 7:12 NIV).
   - What does Matthew 7:12 say to you? And how does it relate to your "Conduct?"
     - _____
     - _____
     - _____

4. "Do to others as you would have them do to you" (Luke 6:31 NIV).
   - What does Luke 6:31 say to you? And how does it relate to your conduct?
     - _____
     - _____
     - _____

5. "When God's people are in need, be ready to help them. Always be eager to practice hospitality" (Romans 12:13 NLT).
   - What does Romans 12:13 say to you? And how does it relate to your conduct?
     - _____
     - _____
     - _____

6. "So, that you may become blameless and pure, children of God without fault in a warped and crooked generation." Then you will shine among them like stars in the sky" (Philippians 2:15 NIV).
   - What does Philippians 2:15 say to you? And how does it relate to your conduct?
   - _____
   - _____
   - _____

7. "I discipline my body like an athlete, training it to do what it should. Otherwise, I fear that after preaching to others I myself might be disqualified" (1 Corinthians 9:27 NLT).
   - What does 1 Corinthians 9:27 say to you? And how does it relate to your conduct?
   - _____
   - _____
   - _____

8. "Make it your goal to live a quiet life, minding your own business and working with your hands, just as we instructed you before" (1 Thessalonians 4:11 NLT).
   - What does 1 Thessalonians 4:11 say to you? And how does it relate to your conduct?
   - _____
   - _____
   - _____

9. "So, that you may live a life worthy of the Lord and please him in every way: bearing fruit in every good work, growing in the knowledge of God" (Colossians 1:10 NIV).
   - What does Colossians 1:10 say to you? And how does it relate to your conduct?
   - _____
   - _____
   - _____

III. Homework Assignment:

This week's homework assignment is to speak only positive and encouraging words. And *conduct* yourself in a manner that brings God glory. Each day find one family member, one friend or a stranger and perform a nice act of service for each of these people each day.

1. **Day One Assignment:**
   a. Speech – Say positive and encouraging things to some-one new each today.
      • Write in the person's name: _____
      • What did you say: _____

   b. Conduct – Conduct yourself in a manner that brings God glory. Perform a nice act of service for two people today.
      • Write in the person's name: _____
      • What was your service: _____
      • Write in the person's name: _____
      • What was your service: _____

2. **Day Two Assignment:**
   a. Speech – Say positive and encouraging things to some-one new each today.
      • Write in the person's name: _____
      • What did you say: _____

   b. Conduct – Conduct yourself in a manner that brings God glory. Perform a nice act of service for two people today.
      • Write in the person's name: _____
      • What was your service: _____
      • Write in the person's name: _____
      • What was your service: _____

3. **Day Three Assignment:**
   a. Speech – Say positive and encouraging things to some-one new each today.
      • Write in the person's name: _____
      • What did you say: _____

    b. Conduct – Conduct yourself in a manner that brings God glory. Perform a nice act of service for two people today.
- Write in the person's name: _____
- What was your service: _____
- Write in the person's name: _____
- What was your service: _____

4. **Day Four Assignment:**
    a. Speech – Say positive and encouraging things to someone new each today.
- Write in the person's name: _____
- What did you say: _____

    b. Conduct – Conduct yourself in a manner that brings God glory. Perform a nice act of service for two people today.
- Write in the person's name: _____
- What was your service: _____
- Write in the person's name: _____
- What was your service: _____

5. **Day Five Assignment:**
    a. Speech – Say positive and encouraging things to someone new each today.
- Write in the person's name: _____
- What did you say: _____

    b. Conduct – Conduct yourself in a manner that brings God glory. Perform a nice act of service for two people today.
- Write in the person's name: _____
- What was your service: _____
- Write in the person's name: _____
- What was your service: _____

6. **Day Six Assignment:**
    a. Speech – Say positive and encouraging things to someone new each today.
- Write in the person's name: _____
- What did you say: _____

b. Conduct – Conduct yourself in a manner that brings God glory. Perform a nice act of service for two people today.
   • Write in the person's name: _____
   • What was your service: _____
   • Write in the person's name: _____
   • What was your service: _____

7. **Day Seven Assignment:**
   a. Speech – Say positive and encouraging things to someone new each today.
      • Write in the person's name: _____
      • What did you say: _____

   b. Conduct – Conduct yourself in a manner that brings God glory. Perform a nice act of service for two people today.
      • Write in the person's name: _____
      • What was your service: _____
      • Write in the person's name: _____
      • What was your service: _____

Prayer:
Lord God please help me to treat people with the love, mercy, and grace you have given to me. Lord let my conduct bring you glory, as I treat people the way I would like to be treated. In Jesus' Name – AMEN.

Session 4: "Love"

First: Open the session with prayer . . .
Second: Check session 3 Homework Assignment . . .

Icebreaker Questions:

1. Tell of a time when you felt love, and how do you know that that person loves you?
2. How can you show someone love without words; how, or why not?

Verse 12: "Don't let anyone look down on you because you are young, but set an example for the believers in speech, in conduct, in *love*, in faith and in purity (1 Timothy 4:12 NIV)."

Timothy was to be an example for *"Love"* for the believers.

Love and in Faith are the Two Cardinal Principles of the Christian; meaning that our love works with faith and our faith works with our love. This means that we should operate with a pure heart, filled with the love of Jesus which we received when He saved us, and gave us a new heart.

So if I asked you do you love your spouse, what would you say? Do you love your mother? Do you love your pet? Do you love ice-cream? Do you love cake? Do you love your chocolate? Do you love your car? We probably would say YES to each question. But we don't love each thing and people at the same level.

However, in America we have only one word for love; therefore, when we say I love _____ . . . what are we really saying?

The Bible or biblical type of love which the believer is to have for people is called *agape love*, which is the great form of love.

Let's look at the types of *biblical Love* . . .

I. **The Types of Love:**
   1. **Agape (noun):** love extended from one to another through a relationship with Jesus Christ. It is the love of God for believers and non-believers.
      a. It is an unconditional love of all individuals.
         - "You see, at just the right time, when we were still powerless, Christ died for the ungodly" (Romans 5:6 NIV).

   2. **Agapao (verb):** expresses a higher type of devotion or a total commitment, the type of love that God the Father has for his children.
      a. It is the love of God for unworthy sinners (all of mankind).
         - "But God demonstrates his own love for us in this: While we were still sinners, Christ died for us" (Romans 5:8 NIV).
      b. It is the love of God for undeserving enemies.
         - "For if, while we were God's enemies, we were reconciled to him through the death of his Son, how much more, having been reconciled, shall we be saved through his life" (Romans 5:10 NIV)!

   3. **Phileo:** It is brotherly love as between siblings or close friends. This is the root for the name of Philadelphia (the City of Brotherly Love).

   4. **Storge:** It is family love, the love from a parent to a child, it is also a love that grows out of friendship.

   5. **Eros:** It's a romantic love, sexual. This is where we get the root of English word erotic.

   6. **Mania:** It is highly emotional love; unstable; the stereotype of romantic love.

   7. **Ludus:** It is love is played as a game; love is playful.

II. What does the Bible have to say about the *Love* of God? Take the time to discuss each verse.

1. John 3:16 (NIV) states: "For God so loved the world, that he gave his only Son, that whoever believes in him should not perish but have eternal life."
   - What does John 3:16 say to you? And how does this type of *love* relate to you?
   - _____
   - _____
   - _____

2. Romans 5:8 (NIV) states: "but God shows his love for us in that while we were still sinners, Christ died for us."
   - What does Romans 5:8 say to you? And how does this type of *love* relate to you?
   - _____
   - _____
   - _____

3. Galatians 2:20 (ESV) states: "I have been crucified with Christ. It is no longer I who live, but Christ who lives in me. And the life I now live in the flesh I live by faith in the Son of God, who loved me and gave himself for me."
   - What does Galatians 2:20 say to you? And how does this type of *love* relate to you?
   - _____
   - _____
   - _____

4. Ephesians 2:4-5 (ESV) states: "But God, being rich in mercy, because of the great love with which he loved us, even when we were dead in our trespasses, made us alive together with Christ— by grace you have been saved."
   - What does Ephesians 2:4-5 say to you? And how does this type of *love* relate to you?
   - _____
   - _____

- _____

5. First John 4:9-11 (ESV) states: "In this the love of God was made manifest among us, that God sent his only Son into the world, so that we might live through him. In this is love, not that we have loved God but that he loved us and sent his Son to be the propitiation for our sins. Beloved, if God so loved us, we also ought to love one another."
   - What does 1 John 4:9-11 say to you? And how does this type of *love* relate to you?
   - _____
   - _____
   - _____

III. What does the Bible have to say about the *Command to Love*? Take the time to discuss each verse.

1. **The Goal** – 1 Timothy 1:5 (NIV): "The goal of this command is love, which comes from a pure heart and a good conscience and a sincere faith."
   - What does 1 Timothy 1:5 say to you? And how does this type of *love* relate to you?
   - _____
   - _____
   - _____

2. **With Action** – 1 John 3:18 (NIV): "Dear children, let us not love with words or speech but with actions and in truth."
   - What does 1 John 3:18 say to you? And how does this type of *love* relate to you?
   - _____
   - _____
   - _____

3. **Show God's Love** – 1 John 4:7-8 (NIV): "Dear friends, let us love one another, for love comes from God. Everyone who loves has been born of God and knows God. [8] Whoever does not love does not know God, because God is love."

- What does 1 John 4:7-8 say to you? And how does this type of *love* relate to you?
  - _____
  - _____
  - _____

4. **Spouse** – 1 Peter 3:7 (ESV): "Likewise, husbands, live with your wives in an understanding way, showing honor to the woman as the weaker vessel, since they are heirs with you of the grace of life, so that your prayers may not be hindered."
   - What does 1 Peter 3:7 say to you? And how does this type of *love* relate to you?
     - _____
     - _____
     - _____

Note: "Loving the people in your house"

5. **Neighbor** – Matthew 22:37-40 (NIV) Jesus replied: "'Love the Lord your God with all your heart and with all your soul and with all your mind.' This is the first and greatest commandment. And the second is like it: 'Love your neighbor as yourself.' All the Law and the Prophets hang on these two commandments."
   - What does Matthew 22:37-40, say to you? And how does this type of *love* relate to you?
     - _____
     - _____
     - _____

Note: This is the people we come in contact with every day (co-workers, team mates, and the people in our neighborhood).

6. **Enemy** – Matthew 5:43-45 (NIV): "You have heard that it was said, 'Love your neighbor and hate your enemy.' But I tell you, love your enemies and pray for those who persecute you, that you may be children of your Father in heaven.

• What does Matthew 5:43-45 say to you? And how does this type of *love* relate to you?

• _____

• _____

• _____

Note: The Bible says that before we were saved, we were enemies of God.

7. **Believers** – 1 John 4:11-12 (NIV): "Dear friends, since God so loved us, we also ought to love one another. No one has ever seen God; but if we love one another, God lives in us and his love is made complete in us."

   • What does 1 John 4:11-12 say to you? And how does this type of *love* relate to you?

• _____

• _____

• _____

Note: We are to Love people throughout the World.

8. **We are to Love the people:** family, friends, neighbors, believers, non-believers and our enemies . . . So how is it you are not to love? And why?

• _____

• _____

• _____

IV. Homework Assignment:

This week's homework assignment is to speak only positive and encouraging words. Display Christian conduct by performing nice acts of service. And you are to show the *love* of God. Each day find one family member, one friend or a stranger and tell them you love them this week (someone new each day).

1. **Day One Assignment:**
   a. Speech – Say positive and encourage things to someone new today.
      • Write in the person's name: _____
      • What did you say: _____

   b. Conduct – Conduct yourself in a manner that brings God glory. Perform a nice act of service for someone new today.
      • Write in the person's name: _____
      • What was your service: _____

   c. Love – showing the love of God. Each day find one family member, one friend or a stranger and tell them you love today.
      • Write in the person's name: _____
      • The act of LOVE: _____
      • Write in the person's name: _____
      • The act of LOVE: _____

2. **Day Two Assignment:**
   a. Speech – Say positive and encourage things to someone new today.
      • Write in the person's name: _____
      • What did you say: _____

   b. Conduct – Conduct yourself in a manner that brings God glory. Perform a nice act of service for someone new today.
      • Write in the person's name: _____
      • What was your service: _____

   c. Love – showing the love of God. Each day find one family member, one friend or a stranger and tell them you love today.
- Write in the person's name: _____
- The act of LOVE: _____
- Write in the person's name: _____
- The act of LOVE: _____

3. **Day Three Assignment:**
   a. Speech – Say positive and encourage things to someone new today.
- Write in the person's name: _____
- What did you say: _____

   b. Conduct – Conduct yourself in a manner that brings God glory. Perform a nice act of service for someone new today.
- Write in the person's name: _____
- What was your service: _____

   c. Love – showing the love of God. Each day find one family member, one friend or a stranger and tell them you love today.
- Write in the person's name: _____
- The act of LOVE: _____
- Write in the person's name: _____
- The act of LOVE: _____

4. **Day Four Assignment:**
   a. Speech – Say positive and encourage things to someone new today.
- Write in the person's name: _____
- What did you say: _____

   b. Conduct – Conduct yourself in a manner that brings God glory. Perform a nice act of service for someone new today.
- Write in the person's name: _____
- What was your service: _____

   c. Love – showing the love of God. Each day find one family member, one friend or a stranger and tell them you love today.
- Write in the person's name: _____
- The act of LOVE: _____
- Write in the person's name: _____
- The act of LOVE: _____

5. **Day Five Assignment:**
   a. Speech – Say positive and encourage things to someone new today.
- Write in the person's name: _____
- What did you say: _____

   b. Conduct – Conduct yourself in a manner that brings God glory. Perform a nice act of service for someone new today.
- Write in the person's name: _____
- What was your service: _____

   c. Love – showing the love of God. Each day find one family member, one friend or a stranger and tell them you love today.
- Write in the person's name: _____
- The act of LOVE: _____
- Write in the person's name: _____
- The act of LOVE: _____

6. **Day Six Assignment:**
   a. Speech – Say positive and encourage things to someone new today.
- Write in the person's name: _____
- What did you say: _____

   b. Conduct – Conduct yourself in a manner that brings God glory. Perform a nice act of service for someone new today.
- Write in the person's name: _____
- What was your service: _____

    c. Love – showing the love of God. Each day find one family member, one friend or a stranger and tell them you love today.
- Write in the person's name: _____
- The act of LOVE: _____
- Write in the person's name: _____
- The act of LOVE: _____

7. **Day Seven Assignment:**
    a. Speech – Say positive and encourage things to someone new today.
- Write in the person's name: _____
- What did you say: _____

    b. Conduct – Conduct yourself in a manner that brings God glory. Perform a nice act of service for someone new today.
- Write in the person's name: _____
- What was your service: _____

    c. Love – showing the love of God. Each day find one family member, one friend or a stranger and tell them you love today.
- Write in the person's name: _____
- The act of LOVE: _____
- Write in the person's name: _____
- The act of LOVE: _____

Prayer:
Lord God, please teach me to love people like you love me. Help me to love the people that treat me wrong with the love you have shown me. Lord let your love flow through me too other for the rest of my life, In Jesus' Name – AMEN.

Session 5: "Faith"

First: Open the session with prayer . . .
Second: Check session 4 homework assignment . . .

Icebreaker Questions:

1. Who is the person you trust the most and why?
2. What is your definition for FAITH?
3. Tell of a time when your faith was tested?

Verse 12: ". . . set an example for the believers in speech, in conduct, in love, in *faith* and in purity" (1 Timothy 4:12 NIV).

Timothy was to be an example of faith; he was called to be faithful and to be loyal to the Lord Jesus Christ.

We must all understand that faith is one of the most important aspects of the Christians life. Because without faith you have nothing; no Savior, no Redeemer and no way to a Holy God.

Faith in God the Father through Jesus means that we reject all other ways of salvation and put our faith in Him alone. The Bible tells us that "salvation is found in no one else, for there is no other name under heaven given to mankind by which we must be saved" (Acts 4:12 NIV). Also, John 14:6 (NIV) states: "Jesus is the only way" . . . it is putting our trusting in Jesus alone.

I. **Faith:** *Take the time to discuss what Faith "Is" and what is Not Faith and the Object of our Faith.*

1. **Faith IS:** "Now faith is confidence in what we hope for and assurance about what we do not see" (Hebrews 11:1 NIV).
   - Faith is trusting or depending on someone or something (the seat you're sitting in).
   - What is this verse saying to you about faith?
   - _____

2. **Faith is NOT:** "And without faith it is impossible to please God, because anyone who comes to him must believe that he exists and that he rewards those who earnestly seek him" (Hebrews 11:6 NIV).
   - The verse states: "without faith it is impossible to please God." What does this mean?
   - _____

3. **The Object of our Faith:** "fixing our eyes on Jesus, the pioneer and perfecter of faith. For the joy set before him he endured the cross, scorning its shame, and sat down at the right hand of the throne of God" (Hebrews 12:2 NIV).
   - We are told to keep our eyes on Jesus. Why is this important?
   - _____

4. **The Power of Faith:** He replied, "If you have faith as small as a mustard seed, you can say to this mulberry tree, 'Be uprooted and planted in the sea,' and it will obey you" (Luke 17:6 NIV).
   - Look at the power of Faith – uproot trees, move mountain (Matthew 17:20 NIV).

5. **Levels of Faith:** *Take the time to discuss each level of Faith*
   a. Little Faith – Matthew 14:31 (NIV) states: "Immediately Jesus reached out his hand and caught him. "You of little faith," he said, "why did you doubt?" (Peter walked on water)
   b. Measure of Faith – Romans 12:3 (NKJV) says: "God hath dealt to every man the measure of faith."
   c. Great Faith – Matthew 8:10 (NIV) tells us: "When Jesus heard this, he was amazed and said to those following him, "Truly I tell you; I have not found anyone in Israel with such great faith."

II. **Types of Faith:** *Take the time to discuss each type of Faith*

1. Supernatural Faith (Saving Faith) – Ephesians 2:8 (NIV): "For it is by grace you have been saved, through faith--and this is not from yourselves, it is the gift of God."
2. The Gift of Faith – 1 Corinthians 12:9 (NIV): "to another faith by the same Spirit, to another gift of healing by that one Spirit,"
3. The Fruit of Faith – Galatians 5:22 (NIV): "But the fruit of the Spirit is love, joy, peace, forbearance, kindness, goodness, faithfulness."
4. Weak Faith – Romans 14:1-2 (NIV): "Accept the one whose faith is weak, without quarreling over disputable matters. One person's faith allows them to eat anything, but another, whose faith is weak, eats only vegetables."
5. Shipwrecked Faith – 1 Timothy 1:19 (NLT): "Cling to your faith in Christ, and keep your conscience clear. For some people have deliberately violated their consciences; as a result, their faith has been shipwrecked."

III. What does the Bible have to say about our *Faith in Action*? Take the time to discuss each verse.

1. "Then he said to them all: ". . . Whoever wants to be my disciple must deny themselves and take up their cross daily and follow me" (Luke 9:23 NIV).
    *   What does Luke 9:23 say to you? And how does it relate to your faith?
    *   _____
    *   _____
    *   _____
    *   What does this verse means – "deny themselves and take up their cross daily"?
    *   _____

2. "Whoever can be trusted with very little can also be trusted with much, and whoever is dishonest with very little will also be dishonest with much." (Luke 16:10 NIV).

- What does Luke 16:10 say to you? And how does it relate to your faith?
  - _____
  - _____
  - _____
- What thing or area of your life God is calling you to be faithful in?
  - _____

3. "Therefore, I urge you, brothers, in view of God's mercy, to offer your bodies as a living sacrifice, holy and pleasing to God--this is your true and proper worship" (Romans 12:1 NIV).
    - What does Romans 12:1 say to you? And how does it relate to your faith?
      - _____
      - _____
      - _____

4. "Therefore, my dear brothers, stand firm. Let nothing move you. Always give yourselves fully to the work of the Lord, because you know that your labor in the Lord is not in vain" (1 Corinthians 15:58 NIV).
    - What does 1 Corinthians 15:58 say to you? And how does it relate to your faith?
      - _____
      - _____
      - _____

5. "Serve wholeheartedly, as if you were serving the Lord, not people," (Ephesians 6:7 NIV).
    - What do Ephesians 6:7 say to you? And how does it relate to your faith?
      - _____
      - _____
      - _____

6. "And we desire that each one of you show the same diligence so as to realize the full assurance of hope until the end,

so that you will not be sluggish, but imitators of those who through faith and patience inherit the promises" (Hebrews 6:11-12 KJV).

- What does Hebrews 6:11-12 say to you? And how does it relate to your faith?

- _____
- _____
- _____

7. "Therefore, my brothers, make every effort to confirm your calling and election. For if you do these things, you will never stumble," (2 Peter 1:10 NIV).

- What does 2 Peter 1:10 say to you? And how does it relate to your faith?

- _____
- _____
- _____

NOTE: The word Election means: "choice" or selection. Election is the act of God before creation, whereby He chose to save us from sin.

8. "So then, dear friends, since you are looking forward to this, make every effort to be found spotless, blameless and at peace with him." (2 Peter 3:14 NIV).

- What does 2 Peter 3:14 say to you? And how does it relate to your faith?

- _____
- _____
- _____

NOTE: "make every effort to be found doing the will of God"

IV. Homework Assignment:

This week's homework assignment is to speak only positive and encouraging words. Display Christian conduct by performing nice acts of service. You are to show the love of God to someone. And, show yourself *faithful* unto God by finding one family member, one friend, or a stranger and tell them how faithful God has been to you or how God has been faithful to someone you know.

Each day find one family member, one friend or a stranger and tell them you love them this week (someone new each day).

1. **Day One Assignment:**
   a. Speech – Say positive and encouraging things to some-one today.
      • Write in the person's name: _____
      • What did you say: _____

   b. Conduct – Conduct yourself in a manner that brings God glory. Perform a nice act of service for someone new today.
      • Write in the person's name: _____
      • What was your service: _____

   c. Love – Showing the love of God. Find someone new and tell them God loves them and that you love them also.
      • Write in the person's name: _____
      • The act of love: _____

   d. Faith – Show yourself faithful to God. This week find one family member, one friend or a stranger and tell them how faithful God has been to you or how God have been faithful in someone you know.
      • Write in the person name: _____
      • The act of faith: _____

2. **Day Two Assignment:**
   a. Speech – Say positive and encouraging things to someone today.
      • Write in the person's name: _____
      • What did you say: _____

   b. Conduct – Conduct yourself in a manner that brings God glory. Perform a nice act of service for someone new today.
      • Write in the person's name: _____
      • What was your service: _____

   c. Love – Showing the love of God. Find someone new and tell them God loves them and that you love them also.
      • Write in the person's name: _____
      • The act of love: _____

   d. Faith – Show yourself faithful to God. This week find one family member, one friend or a stranger and tell them how faithful God has been to you or how God have been faithful in someone you know.
      • Write in the person name: _____
      • The act of faith: _____

3. **Day Three Assignment:**
   a. Speech – Say positive and encouraging things to someone today.
      • Write in the person's name: _____
      • What did you say: _____

   b. Conduct – Conduct yourself in a manner that brings God glory. Perform a nice act of service for someone new today.
      • Write in the person's name: _____
      • What was your service: _____

   c. Love – Showing the love of God. Find someone new and tell them God loves them and that you love them also.
      • Write in the person's name: _____
      • The act of love: _____

d. Faith – Show yourself faithful to God. This week find one family member, one friend or a stranger and tell them how faithful God has been to you or how God have been faithful in someone you know.
*   Write in the person name: _____
*   The act of faith: _____

4. **Day Four Assignment:**
    a. Speech – Say positive and encouraging things to someone today.
    *   Write in the person's name: _____
    *   What did you say: _____

    b. Conduct – Conduct yourself in a manner that brings God glory. Perform a nice act of service for someone new today.
    *   Write in the person's name: _____
    *   What was your service: _____

    c. Love – Showing the love of God. Find someone new and tell them God loves them and that you love them also.
    *   Write in the person's name: _____
    *   The act of love: _____

    d. Faith – Show yourself faithful to God. This week find one family member, one friend or a stranger and tell them how faithful God has been to you or how God have been faithful in someone you know.
    *   Write in the person name: _____
    *   The act of faith: _____

5. **Day Five Assignment:**
    a. Speech – Say positive and encouraging things to someone today.
    *   Write in the person's name: _____
    *   What did you say: _____

    b. Conduct – Conduct yourself in a manner that brings God glory. Perform a nice act of service for someone new today.
- Write in the person's name: _____
- What was your service: _____

    c. Love – Showing the love of God. Find someone new and tell them God loves them and that you love them also.
- Write in the person's name: _____
- The act of love: _____

    d. Faith – Show yourself faithful to God. This week find one family member, one friend or a stranger and tell them how faithful God has been to you or how God have been faithful in someone you know.
- Write in the person name: _____
- The act of faith: _____

6. **Day Six Assignment:**
    a. Speech – Say positive and encouraging things to someone today.
- Write in the person's name: _____
- What did you say: _____

    b. Conduct – Conduct yourself in a manner that brings God glory. Perform a nice act of service for someone new today.
- Write in the person's name: _____
- What was your service: _____

    c. Love – Showing the love of God. Find someone new and tell them God loves them and that you love them also.
- Write in the person's name: _____
- The act of love: _____

    d. Faith – Show yourself faithful to God. This week find one family member, one friend or a stranger and tell them

how faithful God has been to you or how God have been faithful in someone you know.
- Write in the person name: _____
- The act of faith: _____

7. **Day Seven Assignment:**
   a. Speech – Say positive and encouraging things to someone today.
      - Write in the person's name: _____
      - What did you say: _____

   b. Conduct – Conduct yourself in a manner that brings God glory. Perform a nice act of service for someone new today.
      - Write in the person's name: _____
      - What was your service: _____

   c. Love – Showing the love of God. Find someone new and tell them God loves them and that you love them also.
      - Write in the person's name: _____
      - The act of love: _____

   d. Faith – Show yourself faithful to God. This week find one family member, one friend or a stranger and tell them how faithful God has been to you or how God have been faithful in someone you know.
      - Write in the person name: _____
      - The act of faith: _____

Prayer:
Lord God, you are so faithful. You have always kept your promises. You alone have met my every need . . . thank you. Help me through the power of the Holy Spirit to be faithful in my obedience to all of your commands. In Jesus' Name – AMEN.

Session 6: "Purity"

First: Open the session with prayer . . .
Second: Check session 5 homework assignment . . .

Icebreaker Questions:

1. How do you feel when you have your best clothes on?
2. What is your definition for purity?
3. What does the Bible mean when it says, purify yourself?

Verse 12: "Don't let anyone look down on you because you are young, but set an example for the believers in speech, in conduct, in love, in faith and in *purity* (1 Timothy 4:12 NIV)."

As we would look at the world today, we see fornication, adultery, and gay marriage as a norm. However, the Bible has called Christians to live different than the world. Peter tells us in 1 Peter 1:14-16 (NIV): "As obedient children, do not conform to the evil desires you had when you lived in ignorance. But just as he who called you is holy, so be holy in all you do; for it is written: 'Be holy, because I am holy.'" Most people think that purity is something a person has when they are young or a virgin and lose it when they mess up. But that is not what the Bible says; it says that purity is something we are to pursue or go after. It is living life in a manner that would honor Jesus Christ with our mind, body and soul as we faithful obey His commands.

As we look through the Bible, we see that Jesus' life was an example in purity. And here Paul calls Timothy to live a moral, clean, just, honest and pure life.

What is the meaning of the word Purity? Purity is often used in Scripture as a means to communicate holiness or perfection. Purity is freedom from anything that contaminates. Purity is the quality of being faultless, uncompromised, or unadulterated. Such as Pure water is free from anything added, or pure gold that has been refined with all of the dross removed. Sexual purity means to be free from immorality or perversion. A pure life is one in which sin no longer determines and control the individual. But, Purity is important to God, because He said it is, and He alone is truly pure.

I.   What does the Bible to say about your *heart*? Take the time to discuss each verse.

1.   "Blessed are the pure in heart: for they shall see God" (Matthew 5:8 KJV).
     • What does Matthew 5:8 say to you? And how does this verse relate to your purity?
     • _____
     • _____
     • _____

2.   "The goal of this command is love, which comes from a pure heart and a good conscience and a sincere faith" (1 Timothy 1:5 NIV).
     • What does 1 Timothy 1:5 say to you? And how does this verse relate to your purity?
     • _____
     • _____
     • _____

3.   "Do not be hasty in the laying on of hands, and do not share in the sins of others. Keep yourself pure" (1 Timothy 5:22 NIV).
     • What does 1 Timothy 5:22 say to you? And how does this verse relate to your purity?
     • _____
     • _____
     • _____

4.   "So then, dear friends, since you are looking forward to this, make every effort to be found spotless, blameless and at peace with him" (2 Peter 3:14 NIV).
     • What does 2 Peter 3:14 say to you? And how does this verse relate to your purity?
     • _____
     • _____

- _____

5. "Who may ascend into the hill of the LORD? And who may stand in His holy place? He who has clean hands and a pure heart, who has not lifted up his soul to falsehood, and has not sworn deceitfully" (Psalm 24:3-4 ESV).
   - What does Psalm 24:3-4 say to you? And how does this verse relate to your purity?
   - _____
   - _____
   - _____

II. What does the Bible have to say about the *Call to Holiness*? Take the time to discuss each verse.

1. Leviticus 11:44-45 (NIV): "I am the LORD your God; consecrate yourselves and be holy, because I am holy. Do not make yourselves unclean by any creature that moves about on the ground. I am the LORD who brought you up out of Egypt to be your God; therefore, be holy, because I am holy."
   - What does Leviticus 11:44-45 say to you? And how does it verse relate to your purity?
   - _____
   - _____
   - _____

2. Leviticus 19:2 (NIV): "Speak to the entire assembly of Israel and say to them: 'Be holy because I, the LORD your God, am holy.'
   - What does Leviticus 19:2 say to you? And how does this verse relate to your purity?
   - _____
   - _____
   - _____

3. Leviticus 20:7 (NIV): "'Consecrate yourselves and be holy, because I am the LORD your God.'"

- What does Leviticus 20:7 say to you? And how does this verse relate to your purity?

  - _____
  - _____
  - _____

4. Leviticus 20:26 (NIV): "You are to be holy to me because I, the LORD, am holy, and I have set you apart from the nations to be my own."
   - What does Leviticus 20:26 say to you? And how does this verse relate to your purity?

     - _____
     - _____
     - _____

5. First Corinthians 1:2 (NIV): "To the church of God in Corinth, to those sanctified in Christ Jesus and called to be holy, together with all those everywhere who call on the name of our Lord Jesus Christ--their Lord and ours:"
   - What does 1 Corinthians 1:2 say to you? And how does this relate to your purity?

     - _____
     - _____
     - _____

6. Ephesians 1:4 (NIV): "For he chose us in him before the creation of the world to be holy and blameless in his sight."
   - What does Ephesians 1:4 say to you? And how does this verse relate to your purity?

     - _____
     - _____
     - _____

7. First Thessalonians 4:7 (NIV): "For God did not call us to be impure, but to live a holy life."
   - What does 1 Thessalonians 4:7 say to you? And how does this relate to your purity?

     - _____

- _____
- _____

8. Hebrews 12:14 (NIV): "Make every effort to live in peace with all men and to be holy; without holiness, no one will see the Lord."
   - What does Hebrews 12:14 say to you? And how does it relate to your purity?
     - _____
     - _____
     - _____

9. First Peter 1:15-16 (NIV): "Just as he who called you is holy, so be holy in all you do; for it is written: "Be holy, because I am holy."
   - What does 1 Peter 1:15-16 say to you? And how does it relate to your purity?
     - _____
     - _____
     - _____

10. Revelation 22:11 (NIV): "Let him who does wrong continue to do wrong; let him who is vile continue to be vile; let him who does right continue to do right; and let him who is holy continue to be holy."
    - What does Revelation 22:11 say to you? And how does it relate to your purity?
      - _____
      - _____
      - _____

III. Homework Assignment:

This week homework assignment is to speech only positive and encouraging words. Display Christian conduct by performing a nice acts of service. You are to show the love of God to someone. You are to tell people of the faithfulness of God. And, maintain your *purity*, find one family member, one friend or a stranger, and tell them of the Holiness of God.

1. **Day One Assignment:**
   a. Speech – Say positive and encouraging things to some-one today.
      - Write in the person's name: _____
      - What did you say: _____

   b. Conduct – conduct yourself in a manner that brings God glory. Perform a nice act of service for someone new today.
      - Write in the person's name: _____
      - What was your service: _____

   c. Love – showing the love of God. Find someone new and tell them God loves them and that you love them also.
      - Write in the person's name: _____
      - The act of love: _____

   d. Faith – Show yourself faithful to God. Find someone today and tell them how faithful God has been to you or someone you know.
      - Write in the person's name: _____
      - The act of faith: _____

   e. Purity – Be Holy unto God. Tell one family member, one friend or a stranger how God has called us to live a holy life.
      - Write in the person's name: _____
      - What did you say: _____
      - Write in the person's name: _____
      - What did you say: _____

2. **Day Two Assignment:**
   a. Speech – Say positive and encouraging things to some-one today.
      - Write in the person's name: _____
      - What did you say: _____

   b. Conduct – conduct yourself in a manner that brings God glory. Perform a nice act of service for someone new today.
      - Write in the person's name: _____
      - What was your service: _____

   c. Love – showing the love of God. Find someone new and tell them God loves them and that you love them also.
      - Write in the person's name: _____
      - The act of love: _____

   d. Faith – Show yourself faithful to God. Find someone today and tell them how faithful God has been to you or someone you know.
      - Write in the person's name: _____
      - The act of faith: _____

   e. Purity – Be Holy unto God. Tell one family member, one friend or a stranger how God has called us to live a holy life.
      - Write in the person's name: _____
      - What did you say: _____
      - Write in the person's name: _____
      - What did you say: _____

3. **Day Three Assignment:**
   a. Speech – Say positive and encouraging things to some-one today.
      - Write in the person's name: _____
      - What did you say: _____

b. Conduct – conduct yourself in a manner that brings God glory. Perform a nice act of service for someone new today.
    * Write in the person's name: _____
    * What was your service: _____

c. Love – showing the love of God. Find someone new and tell them God loves them and that you love them also.
    * Write in the person's name: _____
    * The act of love: _____

d. Faith – Show yourself faithful to God. Find someone today and tell them how faithful God has been to you or someone you know.
    * Write in the person's name: _____
    * The act of faith: _____

e. Purity – Be Holy unto God. Tell one family member, one friend or a stranger how God has called us to live a holy life.
    * Write in the person's name: _____
    * What did you say: _____
    * Write in the person's name: _____
    * What did you say: _____

4. **Day Four Assignment:**
    a. Speech – Say positive and encouraging things to someone today.
        * Write in the person's name: _____
        * What did you say: _____

    b. Conduct – conduct yourself in a manner that brings God glory. Perform a nice act of service for someone new today.
        * Write in the person's name: _____
        * What was your service: _____

c. Love – showing the love of God. Find someone new and tell them God loves them and that you love them also.
- Write in the person's name: _____
- The act of love: _____

d. Faith – Show yourself faithful to God. Find someone today and tell them how faithful God has been to you or someone you know.
- Write in the person's name: _____
- The act of faith: _____

e. Purity – Be Holy unto God. Tell one family member, one friend or a stranger how God has called us to live a holy life.
- Write in the person's name: _____
- What did you say: _____
- Write in the person's name: _____
- What did you say: _____

5. **Day Five Assignment:**
a. Speech – Say positive and encouraging things to some-one today.
- Write in the person's name: _____
- What did you say: _____

b. Conduct – conduct yourself in a manner that brings God glory. Perform a nice act of service for someone new today.
- Write in the person's name: _____
- What was your service: _____

c. Love – showing the love of God. Find someone new and tell them God loves them and that you love them also.
- Write in the person's name: _____
- The act of love: _____

d. Faith – Show yourself faithful to God. Find someone today and tell them how faithful God has been to you or someone you know.
- Write in the person's name: _____

    • The act of faith: _____

  e. Purity – Be Holy unto God. Tell one family member, one friend or a stranger how God has called us to live a holy life.
    • Write in the person's name: _____
    • What did you say: _____
    • Write in the person's name: _____
    • What did you say: _____

6. **Day Six Assignment:**
  a. Speech – Say positive and encouraging things to some-one today.
    • Write in the person's name: _____
    • What did you say: _____

  b. Conduct – conduct yourself in a manner that brings God glory. Perform a nice act of service for someone new today.
    • Write in the person's name: _____
    • What was your service: _____

  c. Love – showing the love of God. Find someone new and tell them God loves them and that you love them also.
    • Write in the person's name: _____
    • The act of love: _____

  d. Faith – Show yourself faithful to God. Find someone today and tell them how faithful God has been to you or someone you know.
    • Write in the person's name: _____
    • The act of faith: _____

  e. Purity – Be Holy unto God. Tell one family member, one friend or a stranger how God has called us to live a holy life.
    • Write in the person's name: _____
    • What did you say: _____
    • Write in the person's name: _____
    • What did you say: _____

7. **Day Seven Assignment:**

a. Speech – Say positive and encouraging things to some-one today.
   - Write in the person's name: _____
   - What did you say: _____

b. Conduct – conduct yourself in a manner that brings God glory. Perform a nice act of service for someone new today.
   - Write in the person's name: _____
   - What was your service: _____

c. Love – showing the love of God. Find someone new and tell them God loves them and that you love them also.
   - Write in the person's name: _____
   - The act of love: _____

d. Faith – Show yourself faithful to God. Find someone today and tell them how faithful God has been to you or someone you know.
   - Write in the person's name: _____
   - The act of faith: _____

e. Purity – Be Holy unto God. Tell one family member, one friend or a stranger how God has called us to live a holy life.
   - Write in the person's name: _____
   - What did you say: _____
   - Write in the person's name: _____
   - What did you say: _____

Prayer:
Lord God, you are HOLY. You are Purity in all you do. Father please forgive me for all the times I have not shown myself pure . . . body, soul, or spirit. Help me through the power of the Holy Spirit to live my life before you and men in purity that your name may be glorified. In Jesus' Name – AMEN.

Session 7: "The Word of God"

First: Open the session with prayer . . .
Second: Check session 6 homework assignment . . .

Icebreaker Questions:

1. What is your favorite verse or book in the Bible and why?
2. Name two Old Testament books and two New Testament books?
3. How often do you read your bible weekly?

The Word of God . . . Both the Old and New Testament are verbally inspired by God and are inerrant in the original writings. God -The Holy Spirit wrote the Bible, with man as its instrument. Through the providence of God, the Scriptures have been preserved and are the supreme and final authority in faith and life. Second Timothy 3:16-17 (NIV) states: "All Scripture is God-breathed and is useful for teaching, rebuking, correcting and training in righteousness, so that all God's people may be thoroughly equipped for every good work." The Bible is an amazing historical, scientific, and prophetic accuracy of universal influence and life transforming power; all which shows that the Bible could only come from the hand of God.

Verse 13: "Until I come, devote yourself to the public *reading of Scripture*, to preaching and to teaching (1 Timothy 4:13 NIV)."

1. First, Timothy was to study and read the Bible for himself
2. Second, he was to read and preach the Word of God publicly
3. Third, he was to teach the Word of God

Note: The Bible (Scripture) reading is the foundation for all wisdom, understanding, and truth. Matthew 7:24 (NIV) states: "Therefore everyone who hears these words of mine and puts them into practice is like a wise man who built his house on the rock."

I. Study the Word:

1. "Do your best to present yourself to God as one approved, a worker who does not need to be ashamed and who correctly handles the word of truth" (2 Timothy 2:15 NIV).
   - What does 2 Timothy 2:15 say to you? And how does it relate to you studying the Word of God's?
   - _____
   - _____
   - _____

2. "and how from infancy you have known the Holy Scriptures, which are able to make you wise for salvation through faith in Christ Jesus. All Scripture is God-breathed and is useful for teaching, rebuking, correcting and training in righteousness, so that the servant of God may be thoroughly equipped for every good work" (2 Timothy 3:15-17 NIV).
   - What does 2 Timothy 3:15-17 say to you? And how does it relate to you studying the Word of God's?
   - _____
   - _____
   - _____

II. The Words of Jesus about the Word: Take the time to discuss each verse.

1. But he (Jesus) answered, "It is written, "'Man shall not live by bread alone, but by every word that comes from the mouth of God'" (Matthew 4:4 NIV).
   - What does Matthew 4:4 say to you? And how does it relate to you studying the Word of God's?
   - _____
   - _____
   - _____

2. "For truly, I say to you, until heaven and earth pass away, not an iota, not a dot, will pass from the Law until all is accomplished" (Matthew 5:18 ESV).

- What does Matthew 5:18 say to you? And how does it relate to you studying the Word of God's?

- _____
- _____
- _____

III. **The Words of Paul about the Word:** Take the time to discuss each verse.

1. "And we also thank God constantly for this, that when you received the word of God, which you heard from us, you accepted it not as the word of men but as what it really is, the word of God, which is at work in you believers" (1 Thessalonians 2:13 NIV).
   - What does 1 Thessalonians 2:13 say to you? And how does it relate to you studying the Word of God's?

   - _____
   - _____
   - _____

2. "So faith comes from hearing, and hearing through the word of Christ" (Romans 10:17 ESV).
   - What does Romans 10:17 say to you? And how does it relate to you studying the Word of God's?

   - _____
   - _____
   - _____

IV. **The Word of God is** – Other Scriptures: Take the time to discuss each verse.

1. Hebrews 4:12 (NIV): "For the word of God is alive and active. Sharper than any double-edged sword, it penetrates even to dividing soul and spirit, joints and marrow; it judges the thoughts and attitudes of the heart."
   - What does Hebrews 4:12 say to you? And how does it relate to you studying the Word of God's?

   - _____

- _____
- _____

2. Psalm 119:105 (NIV): "Your word is a lamp for my feet, a light on my path."
   - What does Psalm 119:105 say to you? And how does it relate to you studying the Word of God's?
   - _____
   - _____
   - _____

3. James 1:22 (NIV): "Do not merely listen to the word, and so deceive yourselves. Do what it says."
   - What does James 1:22 say to you? And how does it relate to you studying the Word of God's?
   - _____
   - _____
   - _____

4. Luke 11:28 (NIV): He replied, "Blessed rather are those who hear the word of God and obey it."
   - What does Luke 11:28 say to you? And how does it relate to you studying the Word of God's?
   - _____
   - _____
   - _____

5. Matthew 24:35 (NIV): "Heaven and earth will pass away, but my words will never pass away."
   - What does Matthew 24:35 say to you? And how does it relate to you studying the Word of God's?
   - _____
   - _____
   - _____

V. Jesus is the WORD: Take the time to discuss each verse.

1. John 1:1-5 (KJV): "In the beginning was the Word, and the Word was with God, and the Word was God. He was in the beginning with God. All things came into being through Him, and apart from Him nothing came into being that has come into being. In Him was life, and the life was the Light of men. The Light shines in the darkness, and the darkness did not comprehend it."
    *   What does John 1:1-5 say to you? And how does it relate to you studying the Word of God's?
    *   _____
    *   _____
    *   _____

2. *Replace the word, "Word" with the NAME OF JESUS* – In the beginning was *Jesus*, and *Jesus* was with God, and the *Jesus* was God. *Jesus* was with God in the beginning. Through *Jesus* all things were made; without *Jesus,* nothing was made that has been made. In *Jesus* was life, and that life was the light of all mankind. The light (*Jesus*) shines in the darkness, and the darkness has not overcome it.
    *   What does John 1:1-5 say to you? And how does it relate to your and the Word of God's?
    *   _____
    *   _____
    *   _____

3. John 1:14 (BSB): "The Word became flesh and made his dwelling among us. We have seen his glory, the glory of the one and only Son, who came from the Father, full of grace and truth."
    *   What does John 1:14 say to you? And how does it relate to you studying "The God's Word?"
    *   _____
    *   _____
    *   _____

VI. Homework Assignment:

This week homework assignment is to speak only positive and encouraging words. Display Christian conduct by performing nice acts of service. You are to show the love of God to someone. You are to show yourself faithful to God. You are to maintain your Purity. This week you are to complete your daily reading assignments and find one family member, one friend or a stranger and tell someone something you learned from the *Word of God* today.

1. **Day One Assignment:**
   a. Speech – Say positive and encouraging things to some-one today.
      - Write in the person's name: _____
      - What did you say: _____

   b. Conduct – Conduct yourself in a manner that brings God glory. Perform a nice act of service for someone new today.
      - Write in the person's name: _____
      - What was your service: _____

   c. Love – Showing the love of God. Find someone new and tell them God loves them and that you love them also.
      - Write in the person's name: _____
      - The act of love: _____

   d. Faith – Show yourself faithful to God. Find someone today and tell them how faithful God has been to you or someone you know.
      - Write in the person's name: _____
      - The act of faith: _____

   e. Purity – Be Holy unto God. Tell someone how God has called us to live holy life.
      - Write in the person's name: _____
      - What did you say: _____

    f. The Word of God – you are to read these chapters today:
- Genesis – "The Creation Story" – Chapter 1, 2, & 3
- Date: _____, what is your understanding of the chapter?

_____

_____

_____

_____

_____

_____

2. **Day Two Assignment:**

    a. Speech – Say positive and encouraging things to someone today.
- Write in the person's name: _____
- What did you say: _____

    b. Conduct – Conduct yourself in a manner that brings God glory. Perform a nice act of service for someone new today.
- Write in the person's name: _____
- What was your service: _____

    c. Love – Showing the love of God. Find someone new and tell them God loves them and that you love them also.
- Write in the person's name: _____
- The act of love: _____

    d. Faith – Show yourself faithful to God. Find someone today and tell them how faithful God has been to you or someone you know.
- Write in the person's name: _____
- The act of faith: _____

    e. Purity – Be Holy unto God. Tell someone how God has called us to live holy life.
- Write in the person's name: _____
- What did you say: _____

f. The Word of God – you are to read these chapters today:
    • The Gospel of John – "In the beginning" – Chapter 1:1-50
    • Date: _____, what is your understanding of the chapter?

    _____
    _____
    _____
    _____
    _____
    _____

3. **Day Three Assignment:**
   a. Speech – Say positive and encouraging things to someone today.
       • Write in the person's name: _____
       • What did you say: _____

   b. Conduct – Conduct yourself in a manner that brings God glory. Perform a nice act of service for someone new today.
       • Write in the person's name: _____
       • What was your service: _____

   c. Love – Showing the love of God. Find someone new and tell them God loves them and that you love them also.
       • Write in the person's name: _____
       • The act of love: _____

   d. Faith – Show yourself faithful to God. Find someone today and tell them how faithful God has been to you or someone you know.
       • Write in the person's name: _____
       • The act of faith: _____

   e. Purity – Be Holy unto God. Tell someone how God has called us to live holy life.
       • Write in the person's name: _____
       • What did you say: _____

f.   The Word of God – you are to read these chapters today:
   • Romans – "Letter from Paul" – Chapter 8:1-39
   • Date: _____, what is your understanding of the chapter?

_____

_____

_____

_____

_____

_____

4. **Day Four Assignment:**
   a.   Speech – Say positive and encouraging things to someone today.
      • Write in the person's name: _____
      • What did you say: _____

   b.   Conduct – Conduct yourself in a manner that brings God glory. Perform a nice act of service for someone new today.
      • Write in the person's name: _____
      • What was your service: _____

   c.   Love – Showing the love of God. Find someone new and tell them God loves them and that you love them also.
      • Write in the person's name: _____
      • The act of love: _____

   d.   Faith – Show yourself faithful to God. Find someone today and tell them how faithful God has been to you or someone you know.
      • Write in the person's name: _____
      • The act of faith: _____

   e.   Purity – Be Holy unto God. Tell someone how God has called us to live holy life.
      • Write in the person's name: _____
      • What did you say: _____

f. The Word of God – you are to read these chapters today:
    • I John; II John & III John
    • Date: _____, what is your understanding
      of the chapter?

    _____
    _____
    _____
    _____
    _____
    _____

5. **Day Five Assignment:**
   a. Speech – Say positive and encouraging things to some-
       one today.
       • Write in the person's name: _____
       • What did you say: _____

   b. Conduct – Conduct yourself in a manner that brings God
       glory. Perform a nice act of service for someone new
       today.
       • Write in the person's name: _____
       • What was your service: _____

   c. Love – Showing the love of God. Find someone new and
       tell them God loves them and that you love them also.
       • Write in the person's name: _____
       • The act of love: _____

   d. Faith – Show yourself faithful to God. Find someone
       today and tell them how faithful God has been to you or
       someone you know.
       • Write in the person's name: _____
       • The act of faith: _____

   e. Purity – Be Holy unto God. Tell someone how God has
       called us to live holy life.
       • Write in the person's name: _____
       • What did you say: _____

f. The Word of God – you are to read these chapters today:
- Psalms 23 – "The Lord is My Shepherd"
- Date: _____, what is your understanding of the chapter?

_____

_____

_____

_____

_____

_____

6. **Day Six Assignment:**
a. Speech – Say positive and encouraging things to some-one today.
- Write in the person's name: _____
- What did you say: _____

b. Conduct – Conduct yourself in a manner that brings God glory. Perform a nice act of service for someone new today.
- Write in the person's name: _____
- What was your service: _____

c. Love – Showing the love of God. Find someone new and tell them God loves them and that you love them also.
- Write in the person's name: _____
- The act of love: _____

d. Faith – Show yourself faithful to God. Find someone today and tell them how faithful God has been to you or someone you know.
- Write in the person's name: _____
- The act of faith: _____

e. Purity – Be Holy unto God. Tell someone how God has called us to live holy life.
- Write in the person's name: _____
- What did you say: _____

    f.   The Word of God – you are to read these chapters today:
- First Corinthians - The Greatest of These is Love – Chapter 13:1-13
- Date: _____, what is your understanding of the chapter?

_____

_____

_____

_____

_____

_____

7. **Day Seven Assignment:**
   a. Speech – Say positive and encouraging things to some-one today.
   - Write in the person's name: _____
   - What did you say: _____

   b. Conduct – Conduct yourself in a manner that brings God glory. Perform a nice act of service for someone new today.
   - Write in the person's name: _____
   - What was your service: _____

   c. Love – Showing the love of God. Find someone new and tell them God loves them and that you love them also.
   - Write in the person's name: _____
   - The act of love: _____

   d. Faith – Show yourself faithful to God. Find someone today and tell them how faithful God has been to you or someone you know.
   - Write in the person's name: _____
   - The act of faith: _____

   e. Purity – Be Holy unto God. Tell someone how God has called us to live holy life.
   - Write in the person's name: _____
   - What did you say: _____

f. The Word of God – you are to read these chapters today:
- Revelation– The New Heaven and Earth – Chapter 21:1-27
- Date: _____, what is your understanding of the chapter?

_____

_____

_____

_____

_____

_____

Prayer:

Lord God, I thank you for your Word. Your Word is Holy and truth. Father help me to read your Word, understand your Word, but most of all live your Word through the help and power of the Holy Spirit. In Jesus' Name – AMEN.

Session 8: "Spiritual Gifts"

First: Open the session with prayer . . .
Second: Check session 7 homework assignment . . .

Icebreaker Questions:

1. What is the best gift you ever received and what made it the best?
2. What is the difference between a talent and a gift?
3. Do you know what's your spiritual gift is? If so, what is it?

   Note: Our talents and gifts is not for our personal use, but for others. All talents and all spiritual gifts come from God and they are for His glory. A talent can from the genetic makeup of the individual; while a spiritual gift is given only through the power of the Holy Spirit. Both Christians and non-Christians has talents; however only Christians possess spiritual gifts for building the body (Church) of Christ.

Verse 14: "Do not neglect *your gift*, which was given you through a prophetic message when the body of elders laid their hands on you (1 Timothy 4:14 NIV)."

We should understand that God has given every Christian the ability for service.

I. What does the Bible have to say about our *gifts*? Take the time to discuss each verse.

   1. Ephesians 4:11-13 (BSB): It was he who gave some to be apostles, some to be prophets, some to be evangelists, and some to be pastors and teachers, to prepare God's people for works of service, so that the body of Christ may be built up until we all reach unity in the faith and in the knowledge of the Son of God and become mature, attaining to the whole measure of the fullness of Christ.

- What does these verses say to you? And how does it relate to you about your gift?
  - _____
  - _____
  - _____

2. Romans 12:6-8 (NIV): We have different gifts, according to the grace given to each of us. If your gift is prophesying, then prophesy in accordance with your faith; if it is serving, then serve; if it is teaching, then teach; if it is to encourage, then give encouragement; if it is giving, then give generously; if it is to lead, do it diligently; if it is to show mercy, do it cheerfully.
   - What do these verses say to you? And how does it relate to you about your gift?
     - _____
     - _____
     - _____

II. What does the Bible have to say about our different types of Gifts? *Take the time to discuss each gift.*

1. The Prophet: Is the person that gives us the inspired revelation of God's Word.
2. The Pastors /Teachers: Are the people that educate others.
3. The Servants: Are people that serve other by meeting a need.
4. The Givers: Are people that finance the kingdom and bless other in many other ways.
5. The Administration: Are people that can put people in the right area, and get people to work.
6. Exhortations: Are people that are motivator and get people to move.
7. The Person of Mercy: They are the people that love on others (we find that one-third of the people have the gift of mercy).

III. The Importance of knowing your Spiritual Gifts

Spiritual gifts are important because they are a part of our lives, the people around us, and the body of Christ (*the Church*). Therefore, spiritual gifts are a priority in every Christian's life.

1. Spiritual gifts help the Christian understand the will of God for their lives:
   a. God has given each person his or her very own person spiritual gifts; and each person should find out theirs, so you can decide on where and how to serve God.
   b. Also, spiritual gifts will help you set priorities for your life.

2. Spiritual gifts are the outward manifestation of the Holy Spirit:
   a. When we use our spiritual gift, it's allowing the Holy Spirit to minister through us therefore, making us co-laborer with God.
      • 1 Corinthians 3:9 (KJV) states: "For we are laborers together with God."
   b. God/Jesus works through his children to accomplish His will here on earth.

3. Spiritual gifts help fills a deep inner need:
   a. It's called "serving people." Knowing and operating your spiritual gifts will place you in a more fulfilling life than the average person.
   b. Your spiritual gifts can complement and meet an inner need that God has put into every person's soul, Christians and non-Christians alike.

   Note: It has been said, career is what you are paid for; calling (spiritual gifts) is what you are made for.

IV. Why Is It So Important to Developing your Spiritual Gifts?

We should develop our spiritual gift because no one has all the gifts of the spirit, and we all need help in one area or another in our lives.

1. Spiritual gifts help build up the Body of Christ (the Church):
   a. Our spiritual gifts are to influence, to motivate, and build up; Ephesians 4:12 (NIV) states: "to prepare God's people for works of service, so that the body of Christ may be built up."
   b. Our spiritual gifts also complement each other. When the body of Christ operates their spiritual gifts, all its members are healthy and blessed.

2. **Spiritual gifts are for Others:**
   a. We should develop our spiritual gift because our spiritual gifts are for others! Every church has all the spiritual gifts; and with every member operating in his/her gift every need should be met within the body (church)
      • For the Pastors /Teachers – the body needs you to educate us.
      • For the Givers – the body needs you in the area of finance and material blessing.
      • For the person of Mercy – the body needs someone to show us the mercy of the Lord Jesus (They are the people that love on us).
      • We need the person with the gift of exhortations – to motivate us and get us to move.
   b. Most of all, use your gifts in love for the glory of God and the building up of the body (the church), because every Christian has that one gift. First Corinthians 13:13 (NIV) states: "But now faith, hope, love, abide these three; but the greatest of these is love." Always start with love every time you serve, for the glory of God with your spiritual gifts.

"Be a good steward of your gifts!"

V. Spiritual Gifts Test – take the Test in the back of this book on page 137 & 145.

Write in your top two if you have time (page 71). If not discuss it during the next session.

VI. Homework Assignment:

This week's homework assignment is to speak only positive and encouraging words. Display Christian conduct by performing nice acts of service. You are to show the love of God to someone. You are to show yourself faithful to God. You are to maintain your Purity. You are to continue reading new chapters in the Bible and share what you learn. This week you are to identify your *Spiritual Gift* and share your gift with one family member, one friend or a stranger, for the building of the body of Christ and the glory of God.

1. **Day One Assignment:**
   a. Speech – Say positive and encouraging things to someone today.
      • Write in the person's name: _____
      • What did you say: _____

   b. Conduct – Conduct yourself in a manner that brings God glory. Perform a nice act of service for someone new today.
      • Write in the person's name: _____
      • What was your service: _____

   c. Love – Showing the love of God. Find someone new and tell them God loves them and that you love them also.
      • Write in the person's name: _____
      • The act of love: _____

   d. Faith – Show yourself faithful to God. Find someone today and tell them how faithful God has been to you or someone you know.
      • Write in the person's name: _____
      • The act of faith: _____

   e. Purity – Be Holy unto God. Tell someone how God has called us to live a holy life.
      • Write in the person's name: _____
      • What did you say: _____

f. The Word of God – Read a minimum of one NEW chapter today. Tell someone something you learned from the Word of God today.
   - Write in the person's name: _____
   - What did you say: _____
   - New Chapter: _____

g. Spiritual Gift – with your Spiritual Gift Test, list two ways you have found yourself operating in your gift:
   - _____
   - _____

2. **Day Two Assignment:**
   a. Speech – Say positive and encouraging things to some-one today.
      - Write in the person's name: _____
      - What did you say: _____

   b. Conduct – Conduct yourself in a manner that brings God glory. Perform a nice act of service for someone new today.
      - Write in the person's name: _____
      - What was your service: _____

   c. Love – Showing the love of God. Find someone new and tell them God loves them and that you love them also.
      - Write in the person's name: _____
      - The act of love: _____

   d. Faith – Show yourself faithful to God. Find someone today and tell them how faithful God has been to you or someone you know.
      - Write in the person's name: _____
      - The act of faith: _____

   e. Purity – Be Holy unto God. Tell someone how God has called us to live a holy life.
      - Write in the person's name: _____
      - What did you say: _____

f. The Word of God – Read a minimum of one NEW chapter today. Tell someone something you learned from the Word of God today.
    •   Write in the person's name: _____
    •   What did you say: _____
    •   New Chapter: _____

g. Spiritual Gift – with your Spiritual Gift Test, list two ways you have found yourself operating in your gift:
    •   _____
    •   _____

3. **Day Three Assignment:**
    a. Speech – Say positive and encouraging things to someone today.
        •   Write in the person's name: _____
        •   What did you say: _____

    b. Conduct – Conduct yourself in a manner that brings God glory. Perform a nice act of service for someone new today.
        •   Write in the person's name: _____
        •   What was your service: _____

    c. Love – Showing the love of God. Find someone new and tell them God loves them and that you love them also.
        •   Write in the person's name: _____
        •   The act of love: _____

    d. Faith – Show yourself faithful to God. Find someone today and tell them how faithful God has been to you or someone you know.
        •   Write in the person's name: _____
        •   The act of faith: _____

    e. Purity – Be Holy unto God. Tell someone how God has called us to live a holy life.
        •   Write in the person's name: _____
        •   What did you say: _____

    f.   The Word of God – Read a minimum of one NEW chapter today. Tell someone something you learned from the Word of God today.
- Write in the person's name: _____
- What did you say: _____
- New Chapter: _____

    g.   Spiritual Gift – with your Spiritual Gift Test, list two ways you have found yourself operating in your gift:
- _____
- _____

4. Day Four Assignment:

    a.   Speech – Say positive and encouraging things to some-one today.
- Write in the person's name: _____
- What did you say: _____

    b.   Conduct – Conduct yourself in a manner that brings God glory. Perform a nice act of service for someone new today.
- Write in the person's name: _____
- What was your service: _____

    c.   Love – Showing the love of God. Find someone new and tell them God loves them and that you love them also.
- Write in the person's name: _____
- The act of love: _____

    d.   Faith – Show yourself faithful to God. Find someone today and tell them how faithful God has been to you or someone you know.
- Write in the person's name: _____
- The act of faith: _____

    e.   Purity – Be Holy unto God. Tell someone how God has called us to live a holy life.
- Write in the person's name: _____
- What did you say: _____

   f. The Word of God – Read a minimum of one NEW chapter today. Tell someone something you learned from the Word of God today.
- Write in the person's name: _____
- What did you say: _____
- New Chapter: _____

   g. Spiritual Gift – with your Spiritual Gift Test, list two ways you have found yourself operating in your gift:
- _____
- _____

5. **Day Five Assignment:**
   a. Speech – Say positive and encouraging things to someone today.
- Write in the person's name: _____
- What did you say: _____

   b. Conduct – Conduct yourself in a manner that brings God glory. Perform a nice act of service for someone new today.
- Write in the person's name: _____
- What was your service: _____

   c. Love – Showing the love of God. Find someone new and tell them God loves them and that you love them also.
- Write in the person's name: _____
- The act of love: _____

   d. Faith – Show yourself faithful to God. Find someone today and tell them how faithful God has been to you or someone you know.
- Write in the person's name: _____
- The act of faith: _____

   e. Purity – Be Holy unto God. Tell someone how God has called us to live a holy life.
- Write in the person's name: _____
- What did you say: _____

f. The Word of God – Read a minimum of one NEW chapter today. Tell someone something you learned from the Word of God today.
    •   Write in the person's name: _____
    •   What did you say: _____
    •   New Chapter: _____

g. Spiritual Gift – with your Spiritual Gift Test, list two ways you have found yourself operating in your gift:
    •   _____
    •   _____

6. **Day Six Assignment:**
    a. Speech – Say positive and encouraging things to some-one today.
        •   Write in the person's name: _____
        •   What did you say: _____

    b. Conduct – Conduct yourself in a manner that brings God glory. Perform a nice act of service for someone new today.
        •   Write in the person's name: _____
        •   What was your service: _____

    c. Love – Showing the love of God. Find someone new and tell them God loves them and that you love them also.
        •   Write in the person's name: _____
        •   The act of love: _____

    d. Faith – Show yourself faithful to God. Find someone today and tell them how faithful God has been to you or someone you know.
        •   Write in the person's name: _____
        •   The act of faith: _____

    e. Purity – Be Holy unto God. Tell someone how God has called us to live a holy life.
        •   Write in the person's name: _____
        •   What did you say: _____

f. The Word of God – Read a minimum of one NEW chapter today. Tell someone something you learned from the Word of God today.
   - Write in the person's name: _____
   - What did you say: _____
   - New Chapter: _____

g. Spiritual Gift – with your Spiritual Gift Test, list two ways you have found yourself operating in your gift:
   - _____
   - _____

7. **Day Seven Assignment:**
   a. Speech – Say positive and encouraging things to some-one today.
      - Write in the person's name: _____
      - What did you say: _____

   b. Conduct – Conduct yourself in a manner that brings God glory. Perform a nice act of service for someone new today.
      - Write in the person's name: _____
      - What was your service: _____

   c. Love – Showing the love of God. Find someone new and tell them God loves them and that you love them also.
      - Write in the person's name: _____
      - The act of love: _____

   d. Faith – Show yourself faithful to God. Find someone today and tell them how faithful God has been to you or someone you know.
      - Write in the person's name: _____
      - The act of faith: _____

   e. Purity – Be Holy unto God. Tell someone how God has called us to live a holy life.
      - Write in the person's name: _____
      - What did you say: _____

f. The Word of God – Read a minimum of one NEW chapter today. Tell someone something you learned from the Word of God today.
  - Write in the person's name: _____
  - What did you say: _____
  - New Chapter: _____

g. Spiritual Gift – with your Spiritual Gift Test, list two ways you have found yourself operating in your gift:
  - _____
  - _____

VII. Spiritual Gifts Test – take the Test in the back of this book on page 137 & 145.

Write in your top two:
  - _____
  - _____

Prayer:
Lord God, I thank you for the gifts and talents you have given me. I pray that the Holy Spirit would lead me and guide me to use my gift responsibly. I pray that I bring you honor and glory through then. In Jesus' Name – AMEN.

Session 9: "Be Diligent"

First: Open the session with prayer . . .
Second: Check session 8 homework assignment . . .
Third: Discuss each person's Spiritual Gift . . .

Icebreaker Questions:

1. What game, sport or activity have you practiced the most; and why did you practice it?
2. Who is the most consistent person you know?
3. What is the one thing you like to more than anything else, and why?

Verse 15: "*Be diligent* in these matters; give yourself wholly to them, so that everyone may see your progress (1 Timothy 4:15 NIV)."

1. The King James Version of the Bible states: "Meditate upon these thing; give thyself wholly to them; that thy profiting may appear to all."
   a. This means to give oneself totally to the instructions.
   b. This means that we should eat, sleep, and live the instruction from the Word of God.

2. The word diligent comes from the Latin diligere, which means "to value highly, take delight in," but in English it has always meant careful and hard-working.

The *diligence* commanded here echoes the athletic metaphor of verses 7-10, where Christians are urged to train themselves for godliness.

> Have nothing to do with godless myths and old wives' tales; rather, train yourself to be godly. For physical training is of some value, but godliness has value for all things, holding promise for both the present life and the life to come. This is a

trustworthy saying that deserves full acceptance. That is why we labor and strive, because we have put our hope in the living God, who is the Savior of all people, and especially of those who believe (1 Timothy 4:7-10 NIV).

I. What does the Bible have to say about *being diligent*? Take the time to discuss each verse.

1. Second Timothy 2:15 (NIV): Do your best to present yourself to God as one approved, a worker who does not need to be ashamed and who correctly handles the word of truth.
    *   What does 2 Timothy 2:15 say to you? And how does it relate to you being diligent?
        *   _____
        *   _____
        *   _____

2. Second Peter 3:14 (NIV): So then, dear friends, since you are looking forward to this, make every effort to be found spotless, blameless and at peace with him.
    *   What does 2 Peter 3:14 say to you? And how does it relate to you being diligent?
        *   _____
        *   _____
        *   _____

II. **The call of diligent sometimes means to sweat** – Literally; "to be in these things so as to be absorbed in them."

1. Proverbs 21:5 (NIV): The plans of the diligent lead to profit as surely as haste leads to poverty.
    *   What does Proverbs 21:5 say to you? And how does it relate to you being diligent?
        *   _____
        *   _____
        *   _____

2. First Corinthians 10:31 (NIV): So, whether you eat or drink or whatever you do, do it all for the glory of God.
   - What does 1 Corinthians 10:31 say to you? And how does it relate to you being diligent?

   - _____
   - _____
   - _____

III. Give Yourself Wholly:

1. But the sense is intensified by "give yourself wholly to them" or "BE in these things."
2. Timothy is to give all he has — all his life — to being godly, to the ministry of the Word, and to exercising his gift of preaching.
3. 3. Romans 12:1-2 (NIV): Therefore I urge you, brethren, by the mercies of God, to present your bodies a living and holy sacrifice, acceptable to God, which is your spiritual service of worship. And do not be conformed to this world, but be transformed by the renewing of your mind, so that you may prove what the will of God is, that which is good and acceptable and perfect.
   - What does Romans 12:1-2 say to you? And how does it relate to you being diligent?

   - _____
   - _____
   - _____

IV. So, that everyone may see your progress:

1. *It's about God!!!*
2. 2. Matthew 5:14-16 (NIV): "You are the light of the world. A town built on a hill cannot be hidden. Neither do people light a lamp and put it under a bowl. Instead they put it on its stand, and it gives light to everyone in the house. In the same way, let your light shine before others, that they may see your good deeds and glorify your Father in heaven.

- What does Matthew 5:14-16 say to you? And how does it relate to you being diligent?

  - _____
  - _____
  - _____

V. Other People:

1. First Peter 2:12 (NIV): Live such good lives among the pagans that, though they accuse you of doing wrong, they may see your good deeds and glorify God on the day he visits us.

   - What does 1 Peter 2:12 say to you? And how does it relate to you being diligent?

     - _____
     - _____
     - _____

VI. Homework Assignment:

This week's homework assignment is to speak only positive and encouraging words. Display Christian conduct by performing a nice acts of service. You are to show the love of God to someone. You are to show yourself faithful to God. You are to maintain your Purity. You are to continue reading new chapters in the Bible and share what you learn. You are to operate in your Spiritual Gift for the body of Christ and the glory of God. This week you are to demonstrate your commitment to the Lord Jesus Christ by your *diligent.*

1. **Day One Assignment:**
   a. Speech – Say positive and encouraging things to some-one today.
      - Write in the person's name: _____
      - What did you say: _____

   b. Conduct – Conduct yourself in a manner that brings God glory. Perform a nice act of service for someone new today.
      - Write in the person's name: _____
      - What was your service: _____

   c. Love – Showing the love of God. Find someone new and tell them God loves them and that you love them also.
      - Write in the person's name: _____
      - The act of love: _____

   d. Faith – Show yourself faithful to God. Find someone today and tell them how faithful God has been to you or someone you know.
      - Write in the person's name: _____
      - The act of faith: _____

   e. Purity – Be Holy unto God. Tell someone how God has called us to live a holy life.
      - Write in the person's name: _____
      - What did you say: _____

f. The Word of God – Read a minimum of one NEW chapter today. Tell someone something you learned from the Word of God today.
   - Write in the person's name: _____
   - What did you say: _____
   - New Chapter: _____

g. Spiritual Gift – list two occasions you found yourself operating in your gift:
   - _____
   - _____

h. Be Diligent – in all this week's assignment.
   - Speech – Say positive and encouraging things to every person you meet.
   - Conduct – Do something nice for one person this week.
   - Show the love of God to a non-Christian.
   - Tell someone how God has shown Himself faithful to you.
   - Purity – show yourself Holy to God and everyone you meet this week.
   - The Word of God – Read each day.
   - "Be Diligent do not miss any assignment."

2. **Day Two Assignment:**
   a. Speech – Say positive and encouraging things to some-one today.
      - Write in the person's name: _____
      - What did you say: _____

   b. Conduct – Conduct yourself in a manner that brings God glory. Perform a nice act of service for someone new today.
      - Write in the person's name: _____
      - What was your service: _____

c. Love – Showing the love of God. Find someone new and tell them God loves them and that you love them also.
- Write in the person's name: _____
- The act of love: _____

d. Faith – Show yourself faithful to God. Find someone today and tell them how faithful God has been to you or someone you know.
- Write in the person's name: _____
- The act of faith: _____

e. Purity – Be Holy unto God. Tell someone how God has called us to live a holy life.
- Write in the person's name: _____
- What did you say: _____

f. The Word of God – Read a minimum of one NEW chapter today. Tell someone something you learned from the Word of God today.
- Write in the person's name: _____
- What did you say: _____
- New Chapter: _____

g. Spiritual Gift – list two occasions you found yourself operating in your gift:
- _____
- _____

h. Be Diligent – in all this week's assignment.
- Speech – Say positive and encouraging things to every person you meet.
- Conduct – Do something nice for one person this week.
- Show the love of God to a non-Christian.
- Tell someone how God has shown Himself faithful to you.
- Purity – show yourself Holy to God and everyone you meet this week.

- The Word of God – Read each day.
- "Be Diligent do not miss any assignment."

3. **Day Three Assignment:**

a. Speech – Say positive and encouraging things to some-one today.
   - Write in the person's name: _____
   - What did you say: _____

b. Conduct – Conduct yourself in a manner that brings God glory. Perform a nice act of service for someone new today.
   - Write in the person's name: _____
   - What was your service: _____

c. Love – Showing the love of God. Find someone new and tell them God loves them and that you love them also.
   - Write in the person's name: _____
   - The act of love: _____

d. Faith – Show yourself faithful to God. Find someone today and tell them how faithful God has been to you or someone you know.
   - Write in the person's name: _____
   - The act of faith: _____

e. Purity – Be Holy unto God. Tell someone how God has called us to live a holy life.
   - Write in the person's name: _____
   - What did you say: _____

f. The Word of God – Read a minimum of one NEW chapter today. Tell someone something you learned from the Word of God today.
   - Write in the person's name: _____
   - What did you say: _____
   - New Chapter: _____

g. Spiritual Gift – list two occasions you found yourself operating in your gift:
    • _____
    • _____

h. Be Diligent – in all this week's assignment.
    • Speech – Say positive and encouraging things to every person you meet.
    • Conduct – Do something nice for one person this week.
    • Show the love of God to a non-Christian.
    • Tell someone how God has shown Himself faithful to you.
    • Purity – show yourself Holy to God and everyone you meet this week.
    • The Word of God – Read each day.
    • "Be Diligent do not miss any assignment."

4. **Day Four Assignment:**
    a. Speech – Say positive and encouraging things to some-one today.
        • Write in the person's name: _____
        • What did you say: _____

    b. Conduct – Conduct yourself in a manner that brings God glory. Perform a nice act of service for someone new today.
        • Write in the person's name: _____
        • What was your service: _____

    c. Love – Showing the love of God. Find someone new and tell them God loves them and that you love them also.
        • Write in the person's name: _____
        • The act of love: _____

    d. Faith – Show yourself faithful to God. Find someone today and tell them how faithful God has been to you or someone you know.
        • Write in the person's name: _____
        • The act of faith: _____

e. Purity – Be Holy unto God. Tell someone how God has called us to live a holy life.
   • Write in the person's name: _____
   • What did you say: _____

f. The Word of God – Read a minimum of one NEW chapter today. Tell someone something you learned from the Word of God today.
   • Write in the person's name: _____
   • What did you say: _____
   • New Chapter: _____

g. Spiritual Gift – list two occasions you found yourself operating in your gift:
   • _____
   • _____

h. Be Diligent – in all this week's assignment.
   • Speech – Say positive and encouraging things to every person you meet.
   • Conduct – Do something nice for one person this week.
   • Show the love of God to a non-Christian.
   • Tell someone how God has shown Himself faithful to you.
   • Purity – show yourself Holy to God and everyone you meet this week.
   • The Word of God – Read each day.
   • "Be Diligent do not miss any assignment."

5. **Day Five Assignment:**
   a. Speech – Say positive and encouraging things to someone today.
      • Write in the person's name: _____
      • What did you say: _____

b. Conduct – Conduct yourself in a manner that brings God glory. Perform a nice act of service for someone new today.
- Write in the person's name: _____
- What was your service: _____

c. Love – Showing the love of God. Find someone new and tell them God loves them and that you love them also.
- Write in the person's name: _____
- The act of love: _____

d. Faith – Show yourself faithful to God. Find someone today and tell them how faithful God has been to you or someone you know.
- Write in the person's name: _____
- The act of faith: _____

e. Purity – Be Holy unto God. Tell someone how God has called us to live a holy life.
- Write in the person's name: _____
- What did you say: _____

f. The Word of God – Read a minimum of one NEW chapter today. Tell someone something you learned from the Word of God today.
- Write in the person's name: _____
- What did you say: _____
- New Chapter: _____

g. Spiritual Gift – list two occasions you found yourself operating in your gift:
- _____
- _____

h. Be Diligent – in all this week's assignment.
- Speech – Say positive and encouraging things to every person you meet.

- Conduct – Do something nice for one person this week.
- Show the love of God to a non-Christian.
- Tell someone how God has shown Himself faithful to you.
- Purity – show yourself Holy to God and everyone you meet this week.
- The Word of God – Read each day.
- "Be Diligent do not miss any assignment."

6. **Day Six Assignment:**
   a. Speech – Say positive and encouraging things to some-one today.
      - Write in the person's name: _____
      - What did you say: _____

   b. Conduct – Conduct yourself in a manner that brings God glory. Perform a nice act of service for someone new today.
      - Write in the person's name: _____
      - What was your service: _____

   c. Love – Showing the love of God. Find someone new and tell them God loves them and that you love them also.
      - Write in the person's name: _____
      - The act of love: _____

   d. Faith – Show yourself faithful to God. Find someone today and tell them how faithful God has been to you or someone you know.
      - Write in the person's name: _____
      - The act of faith: _____

   e. Purity – Be Holy unto God. Tell someone how God has called us to live a holy life.
      - Write in the person's name: _____
      - What did you say: _____

f. The Word of God – Read a minimum of one NEW chapter today. Tell someone something you learned from the Word of God today.
- Write in the person's name: _____
- What did you say: _____
- New Chapter: _____

g. Spiritual Gift – list two occasions you found yourself operating in your gift:
- _____
- _____

h. Be Diligent – in all this week's assignment.
- Speech – Say positive and encouraging things to every person you meet.
- Conduct – Do something nice for one person this week.
- Show the love of God to a non-Christian.
- Tell someone how God has shown Himself faithful to you.
- Purity – show yourself Holy to God and everyone you meet this week.
- The Word of God – Read each day.
- "Be Diligent do not miss any assignment."

7. **Day Seven Assignment:**
a. Speech – Say positive and encouraging things to some-one today.
- Write in the person's name: _____
- What did you say: _____

b. Conduct – Conduct yourself in a manner that brings God glory. Perform a nice act of service for someone new today.
- Write in the person's name: _____
- What was your service: _____

c. Love – Showing the love of God. Find someone new and tell them God loves them and that you love them also.
- Write in the person's name: _____
- The act of love: _____

d. Faith – Show yourself faithful to God. Find someone today and tell them how faithful God has been to you or someone you know.
- Write in the person's name: _____
- The act of faith: _____

e. Purity – Be Holy unto God. Tell someone how God has called us to live a holy life.
- Write in the person's name: _____
- What did you say: _____

f. The Word of God – Read a minimum of one NEW chapter today. Tell someone something you learned from the Word of God today.
- Write in the person's name: _____
- What did you say: _____
- New Chapter: _____

g. Spiritual Gift – list two occasions you found yourself operating in your gift:
- _____
- _____

h. Be Diligent – in all this week's assignment.
- Speech – Say positive and encouraging things to every person you meet.
- Conduct – Do something nice for one person this week.
- Show the love of God to a non-Christian.
- Tell someone how God has shown Himself faithful to you.
- Purity – show yourself Holy to God and everyone you meet this week.

- The Word of God – Read each day.
- "Be Diligent do not miss any assignment."

Prayer:

Lord God, help me to be diligent and faithful to you, myself, and to the people that are keeping me accountable. Father help me to "BE" the person you have called me to be and help me to make this my lifestyle of bringing you glory. In Jesus' Name – AMEN.

Session 10: "Watch Your Life"

First: Open the session with prayer . . .
Second: Check session 9 homework assignment . . .

Icebreaker Questions:

1. Tell of a time when you or someone else had to be protected?
2. What steps can you take in keeping yourself holy?
3. Who is keeping you accountable and are keeping anyone accountable?

Verse 16: "**Watch your life** and doctrine closely. Persevere in them, because if you do, you will save both yourself and your hearers (1 Timothy 4:16 NIV)."

"Watch your life" refers to the fivefold example of godliness commanded in verse 12:

- in speech
- in life
- in love
- in faith
- in purity

We are to guard our studies and teaching, avoiding the profane doctrines, teachings, notions, philosophies, ideas, and fables of men.

1. Timothy was to flee the temptations that would assault and seduce him. He was to control his thoughts and keeps them pure from the lusts of the world and his flesh. We too should flee the temptations that assault us in every form; otherwise, we will succumb to our immoral thoughts or acts. We are to neither give in to greed nor seek the possessions or wealth of the world.

2. We are to watch our lives for a few reasons:
   - Number one – God is watching us and he will judge our actions.
   - Number two – New Christians need to see a good example of a Christian.
   - And number three – the world needs to see the Word of God being live out!

I. **We are to guard our bodies, keeps it both morally and physically fit:** Take the time to discuss each verse.

   1. First Corinthians 9:27 (KJV): "But I keep under my body, and bring it into subjection: lest that by any means, when I have preached to others, I myself should be a castaway."
      - What does 1 Corinthians 9:27 say to you? And how does it relate to you guarding your life?
      - _____
      - _____
      - _____

   2. First Corinthians 6:19 (NIV): "Do you not know that your bodies are temples of the Holy Spirit, who is in you, whom you have received from God? You are not your own; you were bought at a price. Therefore, honor God with your bodies."
      - What does 1 Corinthians 6:19-20 say to you? And how does it relate to you guarding your life?
      - _____
      - _____
      - _____

   3. First Peter 5:8 (KJV): "Be sober, be vigilant; because your adversary the devil, as a roaring lion, walk about, seeking whom he may devour."
      - What does 1 Peter 5:8 say to you? And how does it relate to you guarding your life?
      - _____
      - _____
      - _____

II. **We are to guard our spirit and keep it spiritually fit.** He worships God every day and lives in God's Word and prayer all day long, and he shares the glorious gospel of Christ, witnessing to and exhorting people as he walks throughout the day.

   1. First Timothy 5:22 (NIV): "Keep thyself pure."
   - What does 1Timothy 5:22 say to you? And how does it relate to you guarding your spirit?
   - _____
   - _____
   - _____

   2. James 1:27 (KJV): "Pure religion and undefiled before God and the Father is this...to keep himself unspotted from the world."
   - What does James 1:27 say to you? And how does it relate to you guarding your spirit?
   - _____
   - _____
   - _____

   3. First Peter 1:13 (KJV): "Wherefore gird up the loins of your mind, be sober, and hope to the end for the grace that is to be brought unto you at the revelation of Jesus Christ."
   - What does 1 Peter 1:13 say to you? And how does it relate to you guarding your spirit?
   - _____
   - _____
   - _____

III. **We are to guard our Heart:**

   1. Philippians 4:7 (NIV): And the peace of God, which transcends all understanding, will guard your hearts and your minds in Christ Jesus.
   - What does Philippians 4:7 say to you? And how does it relate to you guarding your spirit?
   - _____

- _____
- _____

2. Proverbs 4:23 (NIV): Above all else, guard your heart, for everything you do flows from it.
   - What does Proverbs 4:23 say to you? And how does it relate to you guarding your heart?
   - _____
   - _____
   - _____

3. Exodus 23:21 (NIV): Pay attention to him and listen to what he says. Do not rebel against him; he will not forgive your rebellion, since my Name is in him.
   - What does Exodus 23:21 say to you? And how does it relate to you guarding your heart?
   - _____
   - _____
   - _____

IV. We are to guard our Eyes:

1. Proverbs 7:2 (NLT): Obey my commands and live! Guard my instructions as you guard your own eyes.
   - What does Proverbs 7:2 say to you? And how does it relate to you guarding your eyes?
   - _____
   - _____
   - _____

2. Proverbs 17:8 (NLT): Guard me as you would guard your own eyes. Hide me in the shadow of your wings.
   - What does Proverbs 17:8 say to you? And how does it relate to you guarding your eyes?
   - _____
   - _____
   - _____

3. Matthew 6:22-23 (ESV): "The eye is the lamp of the body. So, if your eye is healthy, your whole body will be full of light, but if your eye is bad, your whole body will be full of darkness. If then the light in you is darkness, how great is the darkness!
   • What does Matthew 6:22-23 say to you? And how does it relate to you guarding your eyes?
   • _____
   • _____
   • _____

V. The Word of God States:

1. Matthew 10:22 (NKJV): "He that endures to the end shall be saved."
   • What does Matthew 10:22 say to you? And how does it relate to you guarding your life?
   • _____
   • _____
   • _____

2. Jude 1:21 (NKJV): "Keep yourselves in the love of God, looking for the mercy of our Lord Jesus Christ unto eternal life."
   • What does Jude 1:21 say to you? And how does it relate to you guarding your life?
   • _____
   • _____
   • _____

3. Revelation 3:11 (KJV): "Behold, I come quickly; hold that fast which thou hast, that no man takes thy crown."
   • What does Revelation 3:11 say to you? And how does it relate to you guarding your life?
   • _____
   • _____
   • _____

VI. Homework Assignment:

This week homework assignment is to speech only positive and encouraging words. Display Christian conduct by performing a nice acts of service. You are to show the love of God to someone. You are to show yourself faithful to God. You are to maintain your Purity. You are to continue reading new chapters in the Bible and share what you learn. You are to operate in your Spiritual Gift for the body of Christ and the glory of God. You are to demonstrate your Diligent. This week you are to find two people to hold you accountable, in speech, in life, in love, in faith, in purity and reading the Word of God (please fine season Christians; people with these qualities). *"Watch your Life!"*

1. **Day One Assignment:**
   a. Speech – Say positive and encouraging things to someone today.
      • Write in the person's name: _____
      • What did you say: _____

   b. Conduct – Conduct yourself in a manner that brings God glory. Perform a nice act of service for someone new today.
      • Write in the person's name: _____
      • What was your service: _____

   c. Love – Showing the love of God. Find someone new and tell them God loves them and that you love them also.
      • Write in the person's name: _____
      • The act of love: _____

   d. Faith – Show yourself faithful to God. Find someone today and tell them how faithful God has been to you or someone you know.
      • Write in the person's name: _____
      • The act of faith: _____

e. Purity – Be Holy unto God. Tell someone how God has called us to live a holy life.
   - Write in the person's name: _____
   - What did you say: _____

f. The Word of God – Read a minimum of one NEW chapter today. Tell someone something you learned from the Word of God today.
   - Write in the person's name: _____
   - What did you say: _____
   - New Chapter: _____

g. Spiritual Gift – list two occasions you found yourself operating in your gift:
   - _____
   - _____

h. Be Diligent – in all this weekly assignment.
   - Speech – Say positive and encouraging things to every person you meet.
   - Conduct – Do something nice for one person this week.
   - Show the love of God.
   - Tell someone how God has shown Himself faithful to you.
   - Purity – show yourself Holy to God and everyone you meet this week.
   - The Word of God – Read each day.
   - "Be Diligent do not miss one assignment."

i. Watch your life – find two people to hold you accountable, in speech, in life, in love, in faith, in purity and reading the Word of God (please find seasoned Christians; people with these qualities).
   - Write in the person's name: _____
   - Write in the person's name: _____

2. **Day Two Assignment:**
   a. Speech – Say positive and encouraging things to some-one today.
      • Write in the person's name: _____
      • What did you say: _____

   b. Conduct – Conduct yourself in a manner that brings God glory. Perform a nice act of service for someone new today.
      • Write in the person's name: _____
      • What was your service: _____

   c. Love – Showing the love of God. Find someone new and tell them God loves them and that you love them also.
      • Write in the person's name: _____
      • The act of love: _____

   d. Faith – Show yourself faithful to God. Find someone today and tell them how faithful God has been to you or someone you know.
      • Write in the person's name: _____
      • The act of faith: _____

   e. Purity – Be Holy unto God. Tell someone how God has called us to live a holy life.
      • Write in the person's name: _____
      • What did you say: _____

   f. The Word of God – Read a minimum of one NEW chapter today. Tell someone something you learned from the Word of God today.
      • Write in the person's name: _____
      • What did you say: _____
      • New Chapter: _____

   g. Spiritual Gift – list two occasions you found yourself operating in your gift:
      • _____
      • _____

    h. Be Diligent – in all this weekly assignment.
- Speech – Say positive and encouraging things to every person you meet.
- Conduct – Do something nice for one person this week.
- Show the love of God.
- Tell someone how God has shown Himself faithful to you.
- Purity – show yourself Holy to God and everyone you meet this week.
- The Word of God – Read each day.
- "Be Diligent do not miss one assignment."

    i. Watch your life – find two people to hold you accountable, in speech, in life, in love, in faith, in purity and reading the Word of God (please find seasoned Christians; people with these qualities).
- Write in the person's name: _____
- Write in the person's name: _____

3. **Day Three Assignment:**
    a. Speech – Say positive and encouraging things to someone today.
- Write in the person's name: _____
- What did you say: _____

    b. Conduct – Conduct yourself in a manner that brings God glory. Perform a nice act of service for someone new today.
- Write in the person's name: _____
- What was your service: _____

    c. Love – Showing the love of God. Find someone new and tell them God loves them and that you love them also.
- Write in the person's name: _____
- The act of love: _____

d. Faith – Show yourself faithful to God. Find someone today and tell them how faithful God has been to you or someone you know.
- Write in the person's name: _____
- The act of faith: _____

e. Purity – Be Holy unto God. Tell someone how God has called us to live a holy life.
- Write in the person's name: _____
- What did you say: _____

f. The Word of God – Read a minimum of one NEW chapter today. Tell someone something you learned from the Word of God today.
- Write in the person's name: _____
- What did you say: _____
- New Chapter: _____

g. Spiritual Gift – list two occasions you found yourself operating in your gift:
- _____
- _____

h. Be Diligent – in all this weekly assignment.
- Speech – Say positive and encouraging things to every person you meet.
- Conduct – Do something nice for one person this week.
- Show the love of God.
- Tell someone how God has shown Himself faithful to you.
- Purity – show yourself Holy to God and everyone you meet this week.
- The Word of God – Read each day.
- "Be Diligent do not miss one assignment."

4. **Day Four Assignment:**

a. Speech – Say positive and encouraging things to some-
   one today.
   - Write in the person's name: _____
   - What did you say: _____

b. Conduct – Conduct yourself in a manner that brings God
   glory. Perform a nice act of service for someone new today.
   - Write in the person's name: _____
   - What was your service: _____

c. Love – Showing the love of God. Find someone new and
   tell them God loves them and that you love them also.
   - Write in the person's name: _____
   - The act of love: _____

d. Faith – Show yourself faithful to God. Find someone
   today and tell them how faithful God has been to you or
   someone you know.
   - Write in the person's name: _____
   - The act of faith: _____

e. Purity – Be Holy unto God. Tell someone how God has
   called us to live a holy life.
   - Write in the person's name: _____
   - What did you say: _____

f. The Word of God – Read a minimum of one NEW chapter
   today. Tell someone something you learned from the
   Word of God today.
   - Write in the person's name: _____
   - What did you say: _____
   - New Chapter: _____

g. Spiritual Gift – list two occasions you found yourself
   operating in your gift:
   - _____
   - _____

h. Be Diligent – in all this weekly assignment.
- Speech – Say positive and encouraging things to every person you meet.
- Conduct – Do something nice for one person this week.
- Show the love of God.
- Tell someone how God has shown Himself faithful to you.
- Purity – show yourself Holy to God and everyone you meet this week.
- The Word of God – Read each day.
- "Be Diligent do not miss one assignment."

i. Watch your life – find two people to hold you accountable, in speech, in life, in love, in faith, in purity and reading the Word of God (please find seasoned Christians; people with these qualities).
- Write in the person's name: _____
- Write in the person's name: _____

5. **Day Five Assignment:**
a. Speech – Say positive and encouraging things to some-one today.
- Write in the person's name: _____
- What did you say: _____

b. Conduct – Conduct yourself in a manner that brings God glory. Perform a nice act of service for someone new today.
- Write in the person's name: _____
- What was your service: _____

c. Love – Showing the love of God. Find someone new and tell them God loves them and that you love them also.
- Write in the person's name: _____
- The act of love: _____

d. Faith – Show yourself faithful to God. Find someone today and tell them how faithful God has been to you or someone you know.
   - Write in the person's name: _____
   - The act of faith: _____

e. Purity – Be Holy unto God. Tell someone how God has called us to live a holy life.
   - Write in the person's name: _____
   - What did you say: _____

f. The Word of God – Read a minimum of one NEW chapter today. Tell someone something you learned from the Word of God today.
   - Write in the person's name: _____
   - What did you say: _____
   - New Chapter: _____

g. Spiritual Gift – list two occasions you found yourself operating in your gift:
   - _____
   - _____

h. Be Diligent – in all this weekly assignment.
   - Speech – Say positive and encouraging things to every person you meet.
   - Conduct – Do something nice for one person this week.
   - Show the love of God.
   - Tell someone how God has shown Himself faithful to you.
   - Purity – show yourself Holy to God and everyone you meet this week.
   - The Word of God – Read each day.
   - "Be Diligent do not miss one assignment."

6. **Day Six Assignment:**
   a. Speech – Say positive and encouraging things to someone today.
      • Write in the person's name: _____
      • What did you say: _____

   b. Conduct – Conduct yourself in a manner that brings God glory. Perform a nice act of service for someone new today.
      • Write in the person's name: _____
      • What was your service: _____

   c. Love – Showing the love of God. Find someone new and tell them God loves them and that you love them also.
      • Write in the person's name: _____
      • The act of love: _____

   d. Faith – Show yourself faithful to God. Find someone today and tell them how faithful God has been to you or someone you know.
      • Write in the person's name: _____
      • The act of faith: _____

   e. Purity – Be Holy unto God. Tell someone how God has called us to live a holy life.
      • Write in the person's name: _____
      • What did you say: _____

   f. The Word of God – Read a minimum of one NEW chapter today. Tell someone something you learned from the Word of God today.
      • Write in the person's name: _____
      • What did you say: _____
      • New Chapter: _____

   g. Spiritual Gift – list two occasions you found yourself operating in your gift:
      • _____
      • _____

    h. Be Diligent – in all this weekly assignment.
- Speech – Say positive and encouraging things to every person you meet.
- Conduct – Do something nice for one person this week.
- Show the love of God.
- Tell someone how God has shown Himself faithful to you.
- Purity – show yourself Holy to God and everyone you meet this week.
- The Word of God – Read each day.
- "Be Diligent do not miss one assignment."

7. **Day Seven Assignment:**

    a. Speech – Say positive and encouraging things to someone today.
- Write in the person's name: _____
- What did you say: _____

    b. Conduct – Conduct yourself in a manner that brings God glory. Perform a nice act of service for someone new today.
- Write in the person's name: _____
- What was your service: _____

    c. Love – Showing the love of God. Find someone new and tell them God loves them and that you love them also.
- Write in the person's name: _____
- The act of love: _____

    d. Faith – Show yourself faithful to God. Find someone today and tell them how faithful God has been to you or someone you know.
- Write in the person's name: _____
- The act of faith: _____

e. Purity – Be Holy unto God. Tell someone how God has called us to live a holy life.
  - Write in the person's name: _____
  - What did you say: _____

f. The Word of God – Read a minimum of one NEW chapter today. Tell someone something you learned from the Word of God today.
  - Write in the person's name: _____
  - What did you say: _____
  - New Chapter: _____

g. Spiritual Gift – list two occasions you found yourself operating in your gift:
  - _____
  - _____

h. Be Diligent – in all this weekly assignment.
  - Speech – Say positive and encouraging things to every person you meet.
  - Conduct – Do something nice for one person this week.
  - Show the love of God.
  - Tell someone how God has shown Himself faithful to you.
  - Purity – show yourself Holy to God and everyone you meet this week.
  - The Word of God – Read each day.
  - "Be Diligent do not miss one assignment."

i. Watch your life – find two people to hold you accountable, in speech, in life, in love, in faith, in purity and reading the Word of God (please find seasoned Christians; people with these qualities).
  - Write in the person's name: _____
  - Write in the person's name: _____

Prayer:

Lord God, help me to watch my actions, my tongue, my eyes, my hands, my mind and most of all my heart. Please lead and guard my members to the power of your spirit. Lord let my actions and reaction always bring you joy and glory. In Jesus' Name – AMEN.

Session 11: Watch Your "Doctrine"

First: Open the session with prayer . . .
Second: Check session 10 homework assignment . . .

Icebreaker Questions:

1. What is your definition of Doctrine?
2. Why is Doctrine so important?
3. What would the Christian life be without Doctrine?

Verse 16: "Watch your life and *doctrine* closely. Persevere in them, because if you do, you will save both yourself and your hearers (1 Timothy 4:16 NIV)."

I. What is Doctrine?

1. The word "doctrine" means: "instruction, especially as it applies to lifestyle application." Doctrine is teaching imparted by an authoritative source (www.gotquestions.org).

2. Dictionary.com, states: A particular principle, position, or policy taught or advocated, as of a religion or government, a creed or body of teaching of a religious, political, or philosophical group presented for acceptance or belief; dogma (2015 Dictionary.com, LLC.).

3. The Bible tells us that the entire Word of God is Doctrine! And, it speaks for itself and therefore, we cannot interpret it as we wish. Second Timothy 3:16 (NLT) tells us: "All scripture is given by inspiration of God, and is profitable for doctrine, for reproof, for correction, for instruction in righteousness."

4. Biblical Doctrine helps and teaches us:
   - The nature and character of God.
   - The will of God and His standard of holiness for our lives.

- The path to salvation through faith in Jesus allows.
- Instructions for Christians in the church, work place, home, etc.
- It teaches us that the Word of God is a solid foundation for life.

5. True biblical doctrine is based on the alignment with the character of God, the nature of God, the will of God and the Word of God. True doctrine is the key to spiritual life of success, because what we believe will determine how we live. The more we know about the things of God and his workings, the better we will love Him, and serve Him. The great need today is to have a better understanding of Biblical Doctrine.

6. Biblical Doctrine must be:
   - Scripturally Sound
   - Clear and understandable
   - Evangelical
   - Practical
   - Pliable

7. Biblical Doctrine of is Not:
   - Idle conversation
   - Worldly view
   - Person feelings

Note: We will not see eye to eye in some areas of doctrine and we will have disagreement within the body of Christ and with non-believers. However, our disagreements must not be over the foundation principles of the Christian faith (God the Father, Jesus the Son, the Holy Spirit, The resurrection, EST.). Although things such as, prophecy, the end time, the gifts of the Holy Spirit or the organization of the church are important, they are secondary points of doctrine.

II. Doctrinal Beliefs: (*What WE SHOULD Believe*), what does the Bible have to say about *doctrine*? Take the time to discuss each verse in each section.

1. **The Scriptures:**
   a. Both the Old and New Testament are verbally inspired by God and are inerrant in the original writings.
   b. God - The Holy Spirit wrote the Bible, with man as its instrument. Through the providence of God, the Scriptures have been preserved and are the supreme and final authority in faith and life.
   c. Second Timothy 3:16-17 (NIV) states: "All Scripture is God-breathed and is useful for teaching, rebuking, correcting and training in righteousness, so that all God's people may be thoroughly equipped for every good work."
   d. The Bible is an amazing historical, scientific, and prophetic accuracy of universal influence and life transforming power; all which show that the Bible could only come from the hand of God.

   What are three things you learn from this Doctrine?
   - _____
   - _____
   - _____

2. **God:**
   a. God is unique. No person, object, or idea can compare to God. Therefore, anything we say about God must be based on His revelation of Himself to us.
   b. The reality of God is always much greater than our human minds can understand or express. So, we say that God is "HOLY," the only pure spirit.
   c. There is but one living and true God, who is infinite in being and perfection.
   d. The maker and creator of all things.
   e. God is Omnipotent – all-powerful (Matthew 19:26 NIV)
   f. God is Omniscient– all knowing (Matthew 10:29 NIV)
   g. God is Omnipresent – present everywhere (Psalm 139 NIV).

What are three things you learn from this Doctrine?

- _____
- _____
- _____

3. **Jesus:**
   a. He is the eternal Son of God! The Lord and Savior! The second Person of the Trinity (Philippians 2:5-11 NIV).
   b. The Incarnation of Jesus is that in the one person, there are two natures, a human nature and a divine nature, each in its completeness and integrity. Jesus is the Messiah! He fulfilled God's promises and purpose for His people.
   c. Jesus was God in human flesh led by the Holy Spirit to provide salvation for all men (John 1:14 NIV).
   d. Jesus also continues to minister for us. He ascended to the Father (Acts 1:9 NIV) so He could send the Holy Spirit to be with us (John 16:5-16).
   e. Jesus is seated at the right hand of God as our Priest and Intercessor (Romans 8:34; Hebrews 7:25 NIV). So, in all our troubles we have an advocate pleading for us with the Father.

What are three things you learn from this Doctrine?

- _____
- _____
- _____

4. **Holy Spirit:**
   a. The Holy Spirit is the third person in the Trinity, very God, co-existent with the Father and the Son.
   b. The Holy Spirit was active in creation (Genesis 1:2 NIV) and was known as early as the time of Joseph (Genesis 41:38 NIV).
   c. In the Old Testament, the Holy Spirit in the would come upon individuals so they could perform a task for God.
   d. In the New Testament, Elizabeth and Zachariah were the first two persons to be filled with the Holy Spirit (Luke Chapter 1, verses 41 and 67 NIV).

e. However, the New Testament Holy Spirit was revealed on the Day of Pentecost (Acts 2 NIV), when the Spirit was poured out on all the believers.

f. The Holy Spirit is the chief agent in the regeneration that baptizes the believer into the body of Christ, by His indwelling of an individual.

g. The Holy Spirit convicts us of sin, and a comforter of the believer (Luke 12:12; Romans 15:13 NIV).

What are three things you learn from this Doctrine?
* _____
* _____
* _____

5. **The Trinity:**
   a. "Trinity" is a term not found in the Bible, but the word Trinity is used to describe what is apparent about God in the Scriptures.
   b. The Bible speaks of God the Father, God the Son (Jesus Christ), and God the Holy Spirit. It is also clearly presents there is Only One God.
   c. The term: "Tri" meaning three, and "Unity" meaning one, Tri+Unity = Trinity.
   d. It is a way of acknowledging what the Bible reveals to us about God, that God is yet three "Persons" with the same essence of deity.
   e. There is only one God, but in the unity of the Godhead there are three eternal co-equal Persons, the same in substance, but distinct in their function (Matthew 3:16-17; 28:19 NIV).

What are three things you learn from this Doctrine?
* _____
* _____
* _____

6. **Man:**
   a. Man is the direct creation of God – body, soul, and spirit. Therefore, man is not the result of evolution but is made in the image of God.
   b. "God created man in his own image, in the image of God created he him; male and female created he them" (Genesis 1:27 NIV).
   c. In His image means we can do things God does, such as, talk, rest, sit, walk, hear, smell, reason, think, etc. We even have features as God has, such as, a face and back, a mouth, hands, etc. Yet this does not mean God has the same physical features man has, but that man can function, in part, like God does.
   d. After God created man out of the elements of the earth, He "breathed into his nostrils the breath of life; and man, became a living soul" (Genesis 2:7 NIV).
   e. Because of this divine action, man has both a material and a spiritual nature. The spiritual nature of man reflects his being created in God's image.
   f. This means man has a "spirit and soul and body" (1 Thessalonians 5:23(NIV); Malachi 2:15 (NIV); Matthew 10:28 (NIV).

   What are three things you learn from this Doctrine?
   * _____
   * _____
   * _____

7. **The Soul and Spirit of Man:**
   a. The soul and spirit of man is somewhat similar, but however different.
   b. The Soul is where we make the majority of our decisions.
   c. It is the part of man where intellect comes in; here man can think and reason.
   d. The spirit is part of man's where he can fellowship with God; where life is given.
   e. The Bible tells us that "man must worship in Spirit and in Truth" (John 4:24 NVI), this is where the Spirit of God dwells.

   f. The Scriptures saying God "formed the spirit of man within him" (Zechariah 12:1 ESV) and is "the Father of spirits" (Hebrews 12:9 KJV); that is, the Father of men.

   g. The Bible also tells us: "The body without the spirit is dead" (James 2:26; cf. Judges 15:19; Luke 8:55; 23:46 NIV).

What are three things you learn from this Doctrine?

- _____
- _____
- _____

8. **Satan:**
   a. In Christianity – the Devil or Satan is named Lucifer. An angel who rebelled against God, and has been condemned to the lake of fire and brimstone (Revelation 19:20 KJV).
   b. He is identified in the Bible as:
      - The Serpent in the Garden of Eden (Genesis 3:1 NIV)
      - The Accuser of Job (Job 1; 2 NIV)
      - The Tempter of the Gospels (Matthew 4, Mark 4:15, Luke 8:12 NIV)
      - The Prince of the World (John 14:30 NIV)
      - The father of lies (John 8:44 NIV)
      - And the dragon in the Book of Revelation (Revelation 20:2 NIV)
   c. He is described as hating all humanity, spreading lies, and deceit among the world, and Satan is the accuser Christians before God (Job 1:7-12; 2:3-6; Revelation 12:9-10 NIV).

What are three things you learn from this Doctrine?

- _____
- _____
- _____

9. **Angels:**
   a. The angels are represented throughout the Bible as a body of spiritual beings, and the intermediate or links between God and men.

b. An angel was created by God to be Holy messengers, who delivers God's message of instructions, warnings or hope (Hebrews 1:14 ESV).

c. They are also mighty warriors (Daniel 10:13, 21; Jude 9; Revelation 12:7-9 NIV).

d. Angels are ministering spirits sent to serve those who will inherit salvation (Hebrews 1:14 NIV).

e. An angles has the ability to fellowship with God (Colossians 1:16; Hebrews 1:6 NIV).

f. Angels have intellect, emotion and a will. However, the Bible does not state that angels were created in the image of God, as man.

What are three things you learn from this Doctrine?

- _____
- _____
- _____

10. **Sin:**

a. It is the universal human condition of the broken relationship with God involving missing the mark (Romans 3:23 NIV), to overstep a forbidden line, and breaking Gods instructions, there by falling short of His intention for human life.

b. Sin is doing your will, and not doing the will of God.

c. Sin may be thought of as "anything that robs God of His glory and man of his good."

d. Sin is also a lack of conformity to the moral law of God, by act, disposition (attitude) or condition of mind.

What are three things you learn from this Doctrine?

- _____
- _____
- _____

11. **Gospel:**
    a. The Gospel is the redeeming work of God through the Life, Death, Burial, and the Resurrection of Jesus Christ (1 Corinthians 15:1-28 NIV).
    b. It is the revelation of Gods plan for reconciling man to Himself by forgiving his sin through the person and work of his Son Jesus Christ, which the church has been commissioned to proclaim.
    c. It is sometimes called the Good News of Jesus Christ.

    What are three things you learn from this Doctrine?
    - _____
    - _____
    - _____

12. **Salvation:**
    a. Is deliverance from trouble or evil; it is the process by which God redeems His creation through the life, death, burial, and resurrection of Jesus Christ (Acts 4:12 NIV).
    b. All who, by the grace through faith, receives the Lord Jesus Christ as Savior are born again by the Holy Spirit and become the children of God.
    c. Salvation involves Redemption (1 Peter 1:18-20 NIV), Regeneration (John 3:3; Titus 3:5 NIV), Sanctification (Acts 26:18; Romans 6:1-16 NIV) and Glorification (Romans 8:17; 30 NIV).

    What are three things you learn from this Doctrine?
    - _____
    - _____
    - _____

13. **Grace:**
    a. Grace is God's unmerited favor that provides our salvation.
    b. It could have the acronym; **G**- God, **R**- riches, **A**- at, **C**- Christ, **E**- expense.

c. It is undeserved acceptance and love received from another.

d. It is the attitude of God in providing salvation for sinners (John 3:16 NIV).

e. For the grace of God that brings salvation has appeared to all men (Titus 2:11 NIV).

What are three things you learn from this Doctrine?

- _____
- _____
- _____

14. **The Church:**

a. The local church is a body of believers, with Christ Jesus as the Head and the Holy Spirit as its guide.

b. The universal Church of Jesus Christ is composed solely of those who have been redeemed, regenerated, and sealed by the Holy Spirit and that they are saved to worship and to serve.

c. That it is the responsibility and privilege of all who are saved; to win others to Jesus and they should live a holy life, to separate themselves from and forsake all that might dishonor God, cast discredit on His cause or weaken their testimony (1 Corinthian 1:2 NIV).

What are three things you learn from this Doctrine?

- _____
- _____
- _____

15. **Prophecy:**

a. Prophecy involves disclosing important information that could not have been known to the prophet in any ordinary way.

b. God supernaturally provide prophecy to certain individuals, sometimes known as prophets, by dreams or visions.

c. The Old Testament contains prophecies from various Hebrew prophets who foretold of their people's trials, tribulations and promised blessings.

d. The Book of Revelation in the New Testament is highly accepted as a prophecy related by its author (John) of the events of the end times.

e. We as Christians believe that Jesus fulfilled many prophecies of the Old Testament proving he was the "Son of God", the Messiah, and that He will return in the future to fulfill other prophecies.

f. In the New Testament, the things Jesus told the Samaritan woman about her life (John 4), the information He told the apostles the future (Matthew 24), are examples of prophecy in the Christianity.

What are three things you learn from this Doctrine?

- _____
- _____
- _____

16. **The Lord's Day:**
    a. It is the day that the Lord Jesus Christ was resurrected from the dead and gave us victory over sin and death.
    b. Sunday is the day that is mostly observed by many Christians as the Lord's Day for the regular observances of praise and worship, and as a memorial of the resurrection of Jesus Christ, both privately and publicly.

What are three things you learn from this Doctrine?

- _____
- _____
- _____

17. **The Second Coming:**
    a. Jesus Christ return in power and glory to consummate His work of redemption.
    b. It will be the literal and visible return of Jesus Christ for His Church.

   c. The returning Saviour will stand on the Mount of Olives, causing a great earthquake (Matthew 24:30; Revelation 1:7; 19:11 NIV).

What are three things you learn from this Doctrine?
- _____
- _____
- _____

18. **Marriage:**
   a. The Bible teaches that marriage is ordained by God and is the union between one man and one woman.
   b. The institution of marriage is recorded in Genesis: "The man said, 'This is now bone of my bones and flesh of my flesh; she shall be called "woman," for she was taken out of man.' For this reason, a man will leave his father and mother and be united to his wife, and they will become one flesh" (Genesis 2:23-24 NIV).
   c. God created man and then made woman. God took one of Adam's "ribs" (Genesis 2:21-22 NIV). The Hebrew word for "rib" literally means the side of a person.
   d. The New Testament adds a warning regarding this oneness. "So, they are no longer two, but one. Therefore, what God has joined together, let man not separate" (Matthew 19:6 NIV).

What are three things you learn from this Doctrine?
- _____
- _____
- _____

19. **Sanctity of Life:**
The Bible teaches that all human life is sacred and begins at conception.

   a. The Bible never specifically addresses the word abortion. However, numerous teachings in Scripture make it abundantly clear what God's view of abortion is:

- Jeremiah 1:5 (NIV) tells us that God knows us before He knits us in the womb. "Before I formed you in the womb, I knew you, before you were born, I set you apart; I appointed you as a prophet to the nations."
- Psalm 139:13-16 (BSB) speaks of God's active role in our creation and formation in the womb. "For You formed my inmost being; You knit me together in my mother's womb. I praise You, for I am fearfully and wonderfully made. Marvelous are Your works, and I know this very well. My frame was not hidden from You when I was made in secret, when I was woven together in the depths of the earth. Your eyes saw my unformed body; all my days were written in Your book and ordained for me before one of them came to be."
- Exodus 21:22-25 (BSB) prescribes the same penalty of someone who causes the death of a baby in the womb as the penalty for someone who commits murder. "If men who are fighting strike a pregnant woman and her child is born prematurely, but there is no further injury, he shall surely be fined as the woman's husband demands and as the court allows. But if a serious injury results, then you must require a life for a life— eye for eye, tooth for tooth, hand for hand, foot for foot, burn for burn, wound for wound, and stripe for stripe."

b. This clearly indicates that God considers a baby in the womb as just as much of a human as a full-grown adult.

c. For the Christian, abortion is not a matter of a woman's right to choose; it is a matter of the life or death of a human made in God's image (Genesis 1:26-27; 9:6 NIV).

What are three things you learn from this Doctrine?

- _____
- _____
- _____

III. Homework Assignment:

This week homework assignment is to speech only positive and encouraging words. Display Christian conduct by performing a nice acts of service. You are to show the love of God to someone. You are to show yourself faithful to God. You are to maintain your Purity. You are to continue reading new chapters in the Bible and share what you learn. You are to operate in your Spiritual Gift for the body of Christ and the glory of God. You are to demonstrate your Diligent. You are to watch your life (be held accountable – CHECK-IN). This week you are to watch your *doctrine* closely and memorize the key points of each doctrine as you share them with one family member, one friend and one stranger Christian doctrine.

- *This Doctrine should take more than one week, it's okay, take all the time you need.*

1. **Day One Assignment:**
   a. Speech – Say positive and encouraging things to some-one today.
      - Write in the person's name: _____
      - What did you say: _____

   b. Conduct – Conduct yourself in a manner that brings God glory. Perform a nice act of service for someone new today.
      - Write in the person's name: _____
      - What was your service: _____

   c. Love – Showing the love of God. Find someone new and tell them God loves them and that you love them also.
      - Write in the person's name: _____
      - The act of love: _____

   d. Faith – Show yourself faithful to God. Find someone today and tell them how faithful God has been to you or someone you know.
      - Write in the person's name: _____
      - The act of faith: _____

e. Purity – Be Holy unto God. Tell someone how God has called us to live a holy life.
    *   Write in the person's name: _____
    *   What did you say: _____

f. The Word of God – Read a minimum of one NEW chapter today. Tell someone something you learned from the Word of God today.
    *   Write in the person's name: _____
    *   What did you say: _____
    *   New Chapter: _____

g. Spiritual Gift – list two occasions you found yourself operating in your gift:
    *   _____
    *   _____

h. Be Diligent – in all this weekly assignment.
    *   Speech – Say positive and encouraging things to every person you meet.
    *   Conduct – Do something nice for one person this week.
    *   Show the love of God.
    *   Tell someone how God has shown Himself faithful to you.
    *   Purity – show yourself Holy to God and everyone you meet this week.
    *   The Word of God – Read each day.
    *   "Be Diligent do not miss one assignment."

i. Watch your life – find two people to hold you accountable, in speech, in life, in love, in faith, in purity and reading the Word of God (please fine season Christians; people with these qualities).
    *   Write in the person's name: _____
    *   Write in the person's name: _____

j. Doctrine – memorize the key points of each doctrine. This will make you stronger in your belief and faith. Doctrine will help you defend the faith.

• The Scriptures	• God
• Jesus	• Holy Spirit
• The Trinity	• Man
• The Soul and Spirit of Man	• Satan
• Angels	• Sin
• The Gospel	• Salvation
• Grace	• Prophecy
• The Church	• The Second Coming
• The Day of the Lord	• Marriage
• The Sanctity of Life	

2. **Day Two Assignment:**

a. Speech – Say positive and encouraging things to someone today.
   • Write in the person's name: _____
   • What did you say: _____

b. Conduct – Conduct yourself in a manner that brings God glory. Perform a nice act of service for someone new today.
   • Write in the person's name: _____
   • What was your service: _____

c. Love – Showing the love of God. Find someone new and tell them God loves them and that you love them also.
   • Write in the person's name: _____
   • The act of love: _____

d. Faith – Show yourself faithful to God. Find someone today and tell them how faithful God has been to you or someone you know.
   • Write in the person's name: _____
   • The act of faith: _____

e. Purity – Be Holy unto God. Tell someone how God has called us to live a holy life.
    - Write in the person's name: _____
    - What did you say: _____

f. The Word of God – Read a minimum of one NEW chapter today. Tell someone something you learned from the Word of God today.
    - Write in the person's name: _____
    - What did you say: _____
    - New Chapter: _____

g. Spiritual Gift – list two occasions you found yourself operating in your gift:
    - _____
    - _____

h. Be Diligent – in all this weekly assignment.
    - Speech – Say positive and encouraging things to every person you meet.
    - Conduct – Do something nice for one person this week.
    - Show the love of God.
    - Tell someone how God has shown Himself faithful to you.
    - Purity – show yourself Holy to God and everyone you meet this week.
    - The Word of God – Read each day.
    - "Be Diligent do not miss one assignment."

i. Watch your life – find two people to hold you accountable, in speech, in life, in love, in faith, in purity and reading the Word of God (please fine season Christians; people with these qualities).
    - Write in the person's name: _____
    - Write in the person's name: _____

j. Doctrine – memorize the key points of each doctrine. This will make you stronger in your belief and faith. Doctrine will help you defend the faith.

- The Scriptures
- Jesus
- The Trinity
- The Soul and Spirit of Man
- Angels
- The Gospel
- Grace
- The Church
- The Day of the Lord
- The Sanctity of Life
- God
- Holy Spirit
- Man
- Satan
- Sin
- Salvation
- Prophecy
- The Second Coming
- Marriage

3. **Day Three Assignment:**
   a. Speech – Say positive and encouraging things to someone today.
      - Write in the person's name: _____
      - What did you say: _____

   b. Conduct – Conduct yourself in a manner that brings God glory. Perform a nice act of service for someone new today.
      - Write in the person's name: _____
      - What was your service: _____

   c. Love – Showing the love of God. Find someone new and tell them God loves them and that you love them also.
      - Write in the person's name: _____
      - The act of love: _____

   d. Faith – Show yourself faithful to God. Find someone today and tell them how faithful God has been to you or someone you know.
      - Write in the person's name: _____
      - The act of faith: _____

e. Purity – Be Holy unto God. Tell someone how God has called us to live a holy life.
  • Write in the person's name: _____
  • What did you say: _____

f. The Word of God – Read a minimum of one NEW chapter today. Tell someone something you learned from the Word of God today.
  • Write in the person's name: _____
  • What did you say: _____
  • New Chapter: _____

g. Spiritual Gift – list two occasions you found yourself operating in your gift:
  • _____
  • _____

h. Be Diligent – in all this weekly assignment.
  • Speech – Say positive and encouraging things to every person you meet.
  • Conduct – Do something nice for one person this week.
  • Show the love of God.
  • Tell someone how God has shown Himself faithful to you.
  • Purity – show yourself Holy to God and everyone you meet this week.
  • The Word of God – Read each day.
  • "Be Diligent do not miss one assignment."

i. Watch your life – find two people to hold you accountable, in speech, in life, in love, in faith, in purity and reading the Word of God (please fine season Christians; people with these qualities).
  • Write in the person's name: _____
  • Write in the person's name: _____

j. Doctrine – memorize the key points of each doctrine. This will make you stronger in your belief and faith. Doctrine will help you defend the faith.

- The Scriptures
- Jesus
- The Trinity
- The Soul and Spirit of Man
- Angels
- The Gospel
- Grace
- The Church
- The Day of the Lord
- The Sanctity of Life
- God
- Holy Spirit
- Man
- Satan
- Sin
- Salvation
- Prophecy
- The Second Coming
- Marriage

4. **Day Four Assignment:**
    a. Speech – Say positive and encouraging things to someone today.
        - Write in the person's name: _____
        - What did you say: _____

    b. Conduct – Conduct yourself in a manner that brings God glory. Perform a nice act of service for someone new today.
        - Write in the person's name: _____
        - What was your service: _____

    c. Love – Showing the love of God. Find someone new and tell them God loves them and that you love them also.
        - Write in the person's name: _____
        - The act of love: _____

    d. Faith – Show yourself faithful to God. Find someone today and tell them how faithful God has been to you or someone you know.
        - Write in the person's name: _____
        - The act of faith: _____

e. Purity – Be Holy unto God. Tell someone how God has called us to live a holy life.
- Write in the person's name: _____
- What did you say: _____

f. The Word of God – Read a minimum of one NEW chapter today. Tell someone something you learned from the Word of God today.
- Write in the person's name: _____
- What did you say: _____
- New Chapter: _____

g. Spiritual Gift – list two occasions you found yourself operating in your gift:
- _____
- _____

h. Be Diligent – in all this weekly assignment.
- Speech – Say positive and encouraging things to every person you meet.
- Conduct – Do something nice for one person this week.
- Show the love of God.
- Tell someone how God has shown Himself faithful to you.
- Purity – show yourself Holy to God and everyone you meet this week.
- The Word of God – Read each day.
- "Be Diligent do not miss one assignment."

i. Watch your life – find two people to hold you accountable, in speech, in life, in love, in faith, in purity and reading the Word of God (please fine season Christians; people with these qualities).
- Write in the person's name: _____
- Write in the person's name: _____

j. Doctrine – memorize the key points of each doctrine. This will make you stronger in your belief and faith. Doctrine will help you defend the faith.

- The Scriptures
- Jesus
- The Trinity
- The Soul and Spirit of Man
- Angels
- The Gospel
- Grace
- The Church
- The Day of the Lord
- The Sanctity of Life

- God
- Holy Spirit
- Man
- Satan
- Sin
- Salvation
- Prophecy
- The Second Coming
- Marriage

5. **Day Five Assignment:**

a. Speech – Say positive and encouraging things to someone today.
   - Write in the person's name: _____
   - What did you say: _____

b. Conduct – Conduct yourself in a manner that brings God glory. Perform a nice act of service for someone new today.
   - Write in the person's name: _____
   - What was your service: _____

c. Love – Showing the love of God. Find someone new and tell them God loves them and that you love them also.
   - Write in the person's name: _____
   - The act of love: _____

d. Faith – Show yourself faithful to God. Find someone today and tell them how faithful God has been to you or someone you know.
   - Write in the person's name: _____
   - The act of faith: _____

e. Purity – Be Holy unto God. Tell someone how God has called us to live a holy life.
   - Write in the person's name: _____
   - What did you say: _____

f. The Word of God – Read a minimum of one NEW chapter today. Tell someone something you learned from the Word of God today.
   - Write in the person's name: _____
   - What did you say: _____
   - New Chapter: _____

g. Spiritual Gift – list two occasions you found yourself operating in your gift:
   - _____
   - _____

h. Be Diligent – in all this weekly assignment.
   - Speech – Say positive and encouraging things to every person you meet.
   - Conduct – Do something nice for one person this week.
   - Show the love of God.
   - Tell someone how God has shown Himself faithful to you.
   - Purity – show yourself Holy to God and everyone you meet this week.
   - The Word of God – Read each day.
   - "Be Diligent do not miss one assignment."

i. Watch your life – find two people to hold you accountable, in speech, in life, in love, in faith, in purity and reading the Word of God (please fine season Christians; people with these qualities).
   - Write in the person's name: _____
   - Write in the person's name: _____

j. Doctrine – memorize the key points of each doctrine. This will make you stronger in your belief and faith. Doctrine will help you defend the faith.

• The Scriptures	• God
• Jesus	• Holy Spirit
• The Trinity	• Man
• The Soul and Spirit of Man	• Satan
• Angels	• Sin
• The Gospel	• Salvation
• Grace	• Prophecy
• The Church	• The Second Coming
• The Day of the Lord	• Marriage
• The Sanctity of Life	

6. **Day Six Assignment:**
   a. Speech – Say positive and encouraging things to some-one today.
      • Write in the person's name: _____
      • What did you say: _____

   b. Conduct – Conduct yourself in a manner that brings God glory. Perform a nice act of service for someone new today.
      • Write in the person's name: _____
      • What was your service: _____

   c. Love – Showing the love of God. Find someone new and tell them God loves them and that you love them also.
      • Write in the person's name: _____
      • The act of love: _____

   d. Faith – Show yourself faithful to God. Find someone today and tell them how faithful God has been to you or someone you know.
      • Write in the person's name: _____
      • The act of faith: _____

e. Purity – Be Holy unto God. Tell someone how God has called us to live a holy life.
  - Write in the person's name: _____
  - What did you say: _____

f. The Word of God – Read a minimum of one NEW chapter today. Tell someone something you learned from the Word of God today.
  - Write in the person's name: _____
  - What did you say: _____
  - New Chapter: _____

g. Spiritual Gift – list two occasions you found yourself operating in your gift:
  - _____
  - _____

h. Be Diligent – in all this weekly assignment.
  - Speech – Say positive and encouraging things to every person you meet.
  - Conduct – Do something nice for one person this week.
  - Show the love of God.
  - Tell someone how God has shown Himself faithful to you.
  - Purity – show yourself Holy to God and everyone you meet this week.
  - The Word of God – Read each day.
  - "Be Diligent do not miss one assignment."

i. Watch your life – find two people to hold you accountable, in speech, in life, in love, in faith, in purity and reading the Word of God (please fine season Christians; people with these qualities).
  - Write in the person's name: _____
  - Write in the person's name: _____

7. **Day Seven Assignment:**

a. Speech – Say positive and encouraging things to some-one today.
    - Write in the person's name: _____
    - What did you say: _____

b. Conduct – Conduct yourself in a manner that brings God glory. Perform a nice act of service for someone new today.
    - Write in the person's name: _____
    - What was your service: _____

c. Love – Showing the love of God. Find someone new and tell them God loves them and that you love them also.
    - Write in the person's name: _____
    - The act of love: _____

d. Faith – Show yourself faithful to God. Find someone today and tell them how faithful God has been to you or someone you know.
    - Write in the person's name: _____
    - The act of faith: _____

e. Purity – Be Holy unto God. Tell someone how God has called us to live a holy life.
    - Write in the person's name: _____
    - What did you say: _____

f. The Word of God – Read a minimum of one NEW chapter today. Tell someone something you learned from the Word of God today.
    - Write in the person's name: _____
    - What did you say: _____
    - New Chapter: _____

g. Spiritual Gift – list two occasions you found yourself operating in your gift:

- _____

- _____

h. Be Diligent – in all this weekly assignment.
- Speech – Say positive and encouraging things to every person you meet.
- Conduct – Do something nice for one person this week.
- Show the love of God.
- Tell someone how God has shown Himself faithful to you.
- Purity – show yourself Holy to God and everyone you meet this week.
- The Word of God – Read each day.
- "Be Diligent do not miss one assignment."

i. Watch your life – find two people to hold you accountable, in speech, in life, in love, in faith, in purity and reading the Word of God (please fine season Christians; people with these qualities).
- Write in the person's name: _____
- Write in the person's name: _____

j. Doctrine – memorize the key points of each doctrine. This will make you stronger in your belief and faith. Doctrine will help you defend the faith.

- The Scriptures
- Jesus
- The Trinity
- The Soul and Spirit of Man
- Angels
- The Gospel
- Grace
- The Church
- The Day of the Lord
- The Sanctity of Life
- God
- Holy Spirit
- Man
- Satan
- Sin
- Salvation
- Prophecy
- The Second Coming
- Marriage

IV. Prayer:

Lord God, teach me more about you and your Word, that I may teach others. Jesus please fill me through the power of the Holy Spirit, that retain your Words of truth, and be a light in this wicked world, In Jesus' Name – AMEN.

Session 12: Review Sessions

First: Open the session with prayer . . .
Second: Check session 11 homework assignment . . .

Icebreaker Questions:

1. In what area of your life did you need to change most?
2. What was some of your biggest challenges?
3. What are some steps you have taken and what steps you still need to make?

I. SESSION 1: Overview of the Sessions

We found Paul instructing Timothy; to command all season and mature Christian to teach the new and young Christian how to develop the character of Christ Jesus with the things we find them in First Timothy 4:12-16 (NIV), to speak positive words; how we carry ourselves; the way we show the love of Christ; to be strong in our faith; to live a life of purity; to be a good steward of the Word of God; to be diligent; and to watch our lives and doctrine. Because, this would bring glory to God as we set an example for the believers and unbelievers.

II. SESSION 2: "Speech"

We all have heard it said: "Sticks and Stones may break my bones, but words will never hurt me." This statement in one of the biggest lies every told! Word can hurt! Paul tells Timothy and the Word of God tells us to set an example for the believers in the way he talked; in public and in private. We are to be an example in speech: in what we said and in the way, he said things. We had to control our conversation and tongue no matter the opposition. Remember that "The tongue has the power of life and death" (Proverbs 18:21 NIV).

III. SESSION 3: "Conduct"

Like Timothy, every believer is called to the same high standards of conduct worthy of their honored position in Christ. True believers are to "walk the walk" and "talk the talk" with genuine Christian moral conduct to the glory of God. When we talk about conduct – the word integrity comes to mind. Integrity is a word that is not used much in today's English. One definition of integrity is: "the quality or state of being of sound moral principle; uprightness, honesty, and sincerity" So we can say that a good synonym for integrity is honesty.

IV. SESSION 4: "Love"

"Love" . . . everyone wants it; and we all have abuse it. Paul tells us in first Corinthians 13 that love is: Love is patient, love is kind. It does not envy, it does not boast, it is not proud. It does not dishonor others, it is not self-seeking, it is not easily angered, it keeps no record of wrongs. Love does not delight in evil but rejoices with the truth. It always protects, always trusts, always hopes, always perseveres. Love never fails (1 Corinthians 13:4-8 NIV). God has called every Christian to demonstrate His love to this dying world. Yes, sometimes love hurts, but always remember that "For God so loved the world (YOU) that he gave his one and only Son, that whoever (YOU) believes in him shall not perish but have eternal life" (John 3:16 NIV). Just remember "Love never fails."

V. SESSION 5: "Faith"

We must understand that faith is one of the most important aspect of a Christian's life. Without faith you have nothing; no Savior, no Redeemer and no way to a Holy God. Faith in God the Father through Jesus means to reject all other ways of salvation. The Bible tells us that "salvation is found in no one else, for there is no other name under heaven given to mankind by which we must be saved" (Acts 4:12 NIV). Also, John 14:6 states: Jesus is the only way. Paul tells us in Ephesians, that faith is a gift from God. He states: "For by grace you have been saved through faith. And this is not our own doing; it is the gift of God, not a result of works, so that no one can boast (Ephesians 2:8-9 NIV). He also stated in Romans, "God has given to each person "the" measure of faith (Romans 12:3 NLT). The writer of the book of Hebrews tells us that without faith it is impossible to please God, because we must first believe that He exists. That verse also says that God rewards those who seek him (Hebrews 11:6 NIV). Therefore, we find that the key is the object of our faith – which is Christ Jesus the author and perfecter (finisher) of our faith (Hebrews 12:2 BSB).

VI. SESSION 6: "Purity"

If we would look at the world we would see fornication, adultery, gay marriage as a norm. However, the Bible calls all Christian's to live different then the world does. Peter tells us in 1 Peter 1:14-16 (NIV), "As obedient children, do not conform to the evil desires you had when you lived in ignorance. But just as he who called you is holy, so be holy in all you do; for it is written: 'Be holy, because I am holy.'" When most people thank that purity is something a person has when they are young or a virgin and lose it when they mess up. But that is not what the Bible says; it says that purity is something we are to pursue or go after. It is living life to honor Jesus Christ through our mind, body and soul as we faithful obey His commands.

VII. SESSION 7: "The Word of God"

Both the Old and New Testament are verbally inspired by God and are inerrant in the original writings. God -The Holy Spirit wrote the Bible, with man as its instrument. Through the providence of God, the Scriptures have been preserved and are the supreme and final authority in faith and life. Second Timothy 3:16-17 (NIV) states, "All Scripture is God-breathed and is useful for teaching, rebuking, correcting and training in righteousness, so that all God's people may be thoroughly equipped for every good work." The Bible is an amazing historical, scientific, and prophetic accuracy of universal influence and life transforming power; all which shows that the Bible could only come from the hand of God.

VIII. SESSION 8: "Spiritual Gifts"

Spiritual Gifts are given by the Holy Spirit to Christians for the purpose of building up the body of Christ (the Church). Remember that our talents and gifts is not for our personal use, but for others. All talents and spiritual gifts come from God and they are for His glory. A talent can from the genetic makeup of the individual; while a spiritual gift is given only through the power of the Holy Spirit. Both Christians and non-Christians has talents, but only Christians has spiritual gifts from the Holy Spirit.

IX. SESSION 9: "Be Diligent"

The call to be diligent is a call to be faithful; to give oneself totally to the instructions of the Word of God. This means we should eat, sleep, and live the way God has commanded us. The word diligent comes from the Latin *diligere*, which means "to value highly, take delight in;" but in English it has always meant careful and hard-working. Paul tells us why we should be diligent; in the third part of verse 15, (First Timothy Four) he states: "so that everyone may see your progress". The way Christians live is critical, because it can and will affect the salvation of the people we are surrounded. This will always bring glory to the Lord Jesus Christ.

X. SESSION 10: "Watch Your Life"

The call to "Watch your life" refers to the fivefold example of godliness which is commanded in verse 12 (First Timothy Four) which is our speech, the way we live, how we demonstrate love, our faith in God, and our life of purity. We must be on constant guard against falling into sin that can destroy the name of Jesus Christ, His church, and our testimonies. Also, we are to watch our lives because God is watching us and he will judge our actions. The third reason is that the new Christian need to see a good example of a real Christian. And fourth reason is, the world needs to see the Word of God being live out! Again . . . the way we live our lives can be a great sermon to those around us, because it allows them to see the Jesus in you!

XI. SESSION 11: Watch Your "Doctrine"

Doctrine is simply beliefs or teachings; doctrine is instruction, as it applies to one's lifestyle application; doctrine is particular principle, position of a religion or government, teaching of a religious, political, or philosophical group presented for acceptance or belief. The Bible tells us that the entire Word of God is DOCTRINE! And, it speaks for itself and therefore, we cannot interpret it as we wish. Second Timothy 3:16 (ESV) tells us, "All scripture is given by inspiration of God, and is profitable for doctrine, for reproof, for correction, for instruction in righteousness." True biblical doctrine is based on the alignment with the character of God, the nature of God, the will of God and the Word of God. Biblical Doctrine is scriptural sound, clear and understandable, evangelical, practical, pliable. Biblical Doctrine of is not idle conversation, worldly view or person feelings. Biblical Doctrine teaches us truth!

SPIRITUAL GIFTS TEST
YOUTH SPIRITUAL GIFTS TEST

How to take this test:

Romans 12:3 (ESV) says, "For by the grace given to me I say to everyone among you not to think of himself more highly than he ought to think, but to think with sober judgment, each according to the measure of faith that God has assigned."

For the best results answer each statement below according to who you are, not who you would like to be or think you ought to be. How true are these statements of you? What has been your experience? What do others tell you? To what degree do these statements reflect your usual tendencies? Each question is very important, so try not to miss out on any. Your score is calculated at the end of the test.

Respond to each statement according to this 0-5-point scale:

0 = Never; Not true
1 = Rarely; Seldom true
2 = Sometime; Occasionally true
3 = Half of the time; Usually true
4 = Most of the time; Consistently true
5 = All of the time; Always true

Begin:

1. _____ I can organize my friends or classmates to accomplish a goal or task.

2. _____ I can tell if a statement is from the Bible or not.

3. _____ I have a good understanding of the Gospel, and can easily share it with others.

4. _____ I believe everyone needs encouragement in this life, and I love to give it.

5. _____ I have great confidence that God is personally and deeply involved with my life.

6. _____ I don't spend my money on things I don't need so I can give more of it to God.

7. _____ I have big dreams to live my life for God.

8. _____ I have compassion for those who are having hard times in their lives.

9. _____ I always pray for other people.

10. _____ I enjoy doing everyday tasks that support the different ministries of the church.

11. _____ I often spend time a lot of time studying the Bible so I can make a difference in someone's life.

12. _____ I can easily create a plan and put it into place to get something done.

13. _____ I listen carefully to what people say and teach to see if it is true or not.

14. _____ My heart is heavy for those who are lost without Jesus.

15. _____ When I see someone, who is discouraged, I remind them of how great God is and how much He has promised to take care of them.

16. _____ I trust God completely to answer my prayers according to His perfect will.

17. _____ I love giving money to help the Church share the Gospel.

18. _____ I like to set goals and reach them, even if others oppose them.

19. _____ I see the sick or needy as those who most need the love and comfort that Jesus offers.

20. _____ I love helping others learn and grow in their faith.

21. _____ I gladly volunteer to help in church when I know it will fill a practical need.

22. _____ When I teach the Bible, others are interested and want to learn more.

23. _____ When I am in a group, I clearly see how everyone can contribute to accomplish our goal together.

24. _____ I can tell easily if a person is phony or fake.

25. _____ I always look for opportunities to build relationships with non-Christians.

26. _____ I feel God pushing me to inspire those who are not growing in their faith.

27. _____ I know God will come through even if I don't see how He will do it.

28. _____ It makes me happy knowing that when I give to the Church people will be helped and told about Jesus.

29. _____ I am not afraid to take risks to advance the kingdom of God.

30. _____ I care deeply about those who are hurting and want to help them through their tough times.

31. _____ Relationships are very important to me. I am definitely a "people person."

32. _____ I like to be in the background and have no need of recognition when I serve in the church.

33. _____ I enjoy explaining things to people so they can grow spiritually and personally.

34. _____ I organize things so my life runs more smoothly.

35. _____ I can decide quickly if there is an evil or wicked influence in a situation.

36. _____ I love to memorize Bible verses to share with those who don't know Jesus as their Savior.

37. _____ I am not afraid to challenge someone if I know it will inspire spiritual growth and boldness in their life.

38. _____ I will boldly step out in faith if I sense God is telling me to do something.

39. _____ Even though I give a good portion of what I have to God, He still blesses me with more than I need.

40. _____ I love to help others grow in their gifts and abilities.

41. _____ I love to help people through the problems of life and show them the compassion that Jesus did.

42. _____ I care about the church and want to see it grow and be built up in love.

43. _____ I set aside time and try to help those in need around me.

44. _____ I hate it when someone uses Bible verses out of context for their own purposes.

45. _____ I care about the details when I am working on something.

46. _____ I can usually tell if someone is being deceitful or dishonest before anyone else can.

47. _____ I love to share what Christ has done in my life and how He has changed me.

48. _____ Others have told me that my encouraging words have helped them to step out and grow in their faith.

49. _____ Even when times are tough, I trust that God will comfort me and provide for my needs.

50. _____ I want to make God happy with how I use my money.

51. _____ People often look to me to lead a group or project at school or church.

52. _____ I have been known to "care too much" and help others in their time of need.

53. _____ I want to see everyone in the church fulfilling the Great Commission.

54. _____ If I see a need in the church I simply fill it without being asked.

55. _____ I pay attention to the words people use because each word is significant and has meaning.

56. _____ I know how to manage my time to get my daily work done.

57. _____ I see things plainly as good or evil, right or wrong, true or false.

58. _____ I feel I have to tell my friends about Jesus, especially those who don't go to church.

59. _____ When others are faced with difficult problems, I confidently reassure them of God's faithfulness towards His people.

60. _____ I rarely worry because I know God is strong and will help me through every problem.

61. _____ I look for ways to personally help the poor and needy.

62. _____ I am not afraid to step up and take charge in a difficult situation.

63. _____ I look for those who are "outcasts" and help them put their lives back together.

64. _____ The Gospel of Jesus Christ is the most important thing in my life and ministry.

65. _____ I believe there is eternal importance in doing ordinary jobs at church.

66. _____ When I study the Bible, I am always finding out new interesting things about the Gospel.

67. _____ My room is always clean and in order.

68. _____ Others have told me I am a good judge of character.

69. _____ Most of my conversations with non-Christians lead to me speaking about my faith in Jesus.

70. _____ If I see people stumbling in their faith, I encourage them to remember what God has done and come back to the joy He offers us.

71. _____ I always encourage others to trust God in everything.

72. _____ When I get a paycheck or allowance, the first thing I do is ask God - what He wants me to give.

73. _____ I concentrate more on the big picture than the small details.

74. _____ Others have said that I have comforted them at a low point in their lives.

75. _____ I do not seek the "spotlight," but I believe God is preparing me to minister to others.

76. _____ I find joy in being a helper and assisting others in their ministries.

77. _____ Often the Holy Spirit gives me just the right words to say when I am teaching something.

Scoring Directions:

Write your score (from 0-5) for each question in the box with that question number. Add up each column and write your total scores above the corresponding Gift Code. Once you have done this you can check the key below to see what spiritual gift each Gift Code represents. The highest score for any gift is 35. The higher the score, the stronger you are in that spiritual gift based on your responses.

Scoring Matrix

1	2	3	4	5	6	7	8	9	10	11
12	13	14	15	16	17	18	19	20	21	22
23	24	25	26	27	28	29	30	31	32	33
34	35	36	37	38	39	40	41	42	43	44
45	46	47	48	49	50	51	52	53	54	55
56	57	58	59	60	61	62	63	64	65	66
67	68	69	70	71	72	73	74	75	76	77
Total Scores										
Gift Codes Ad	Di	Ev	Ex	Fa	Gi	Le	Me	Pa	Se	Te

Gift Codes:

Ad = Administration **Di** = Discernment **Ev** = Evangelism **Ex** = Exhortation
Fa = Faith **Gi** = Giving **Le** = Leadership **Me** = Mercy **Pa** = Pastor/ Shepherd
Se = Serving/Ministering **Te** = Teaching

SPIRITUAL GIFTS TEST
Adult Spiritual Gifts Test

How to take this test:

Romans 12:3 says, "For by the grace given to me I say to everyone among you not to think of himself more highly than he ought to think, but to think with sober judgment, each according to the measure of faith that God has assigned."

For the best results answer each statement below according to who you are, not who you would like to be or think you ought to be. How true are these statements of you? What has been your experience? What do others tell you? To what degree do these statements reflect your usual tendencies? Each question is very important, so try not to miss out on any. Your score is calculated at the end of the test.

Respond to each statement according to this 0-5-point scale:

0 = Never; Not true
1 = Rarely; Seldom true
2 = Sometime; Occasionally true
3 = Half of the time; Usually true
4 = Most of the time; Consistently true
5 = All of the time; Always true

Begin:

1. _____ I am skilled at organizing people to accomplish many different tasks and objectives.

2. _____ I like to venture out and start new projects.

3. _____ I can easily determine whether a statement is true to Scripture or not.

4. _____ I can clearly and effectively communicate the Gospel to others.

5. _____ I believe everyone needs encouragement in this life, and I love to give it.

6. _____ I live confidently knowing that God is intimately concerned and involved with my life.

7. _____ I live a simple lifestyle so I can give a larger portion of my income to The Lord's work.

8. _____ People often ask me my perspective or interpretation of specific passages of Scripture.

9. _____ I have been told that I am a "dreamer."

10. _____ I have great empathy for those who are facing difficult life challenges.

11. _____ I am very protective of the spiritual well-being of others.

12. _____ At times God, has given me a message for an individual or group and compelled me to speak it to them.

13. _____ I enjoy doing everyday tasks that support the various ministries of the church.

14. _____ I spend large amounts of time studying the Word of God knowing that my effort will make a difference in someone's life.

15. _____ I often have helpful insights into situations that have not been made clear to others.

16. _____ I can clearly see what needs to be done and implement a plan to make it happen.

17. _____ I am willing to take risks for the kingdom of God that others may not.

18. _____ I pay attention to what people say and how they say it, particularly those who teach.

19. _____ I feel a burden of compassion for those who are lost without Jesus.

20. _____ When people are discouraged, I remind them of the power and promises of God found in Scripture.

21. _____ I trust God completely to answer my prayers according to His perfect will.

22. _____ I consistently and joyfully give of my income - often more than a tithe.

23. _____ The Spirit has brought to my mind information that I have been able to use to minister to others effectively.

24. _____ I have a vision for my church or ministry and I know what needs to be done to accomplish it.

25. _____ I see the sick or needy as those who most need the love and comfort that Jesus offers.

26. _____ I love spending time nurturing and guiding others in their faith.

27. _____ There have been occasions that I have received a revelation from the Lord and spoken it to the church.

28. _____ I readily volunteer to help in church when I know it will fill a practical need.

29. _____ I effectively communicate the Bible in ways that influence and motivate others to learn more.

30. _____ I have learned through my experiences in life and can often guide others who are facing similar difficulties or challenges that I have had.

31. _____ I am good at delegating responsibility and trust others to "do their jobs."

32. _____ I can minister to people in different cultures effectively.

33. _____ I am a quick and accurate judge of character.

34. _____ I seek ways to build relationships with non-Christians so that The Lord will use me to share the Gospel with them.

35. _____ I am compelled to challenge and inspire growth in those whose faith is stagnant.

36. _____ I know God will come through even if I don't see any possible solution to my problem.

37. _____ When I give, it brings me great joy knowing that more people will be served and touched with the Gospel.

38. _____ I study the Bible regularly in order to share truth with others in and outside the church.

39. _____ I am not afraid to take risks to advance the kingdom of God through my church or ministry.

40. _____ I care deeply about those who are hurting and want to help them navigate through their tough times.

41. _____ I desire to help the wounded and lost find healing and shelter in Jesus Christ.

42. _____ The Lord has spontaneously given me information about an individual that I felt obligated to confront them with in order to restore them to God.

43. _____ I like to be in the background and have no need of recognition for my service in the church.

44. _____ I am able to explain deep theological truths in ways that even a child can understand them.

45. _____ I often help people by offering Scriptural lessons and principles as solutions to life's various challenges.

46. _____ I like to create ways to make things run efficiently in my life and work.

47. _____ God has given me influence over several different ministries and/or churches.

48. _____ I can readily sense the enemy or a demonic influence in a situation.

49. _____ I love to memorize Scripture to share with those who don't know Jesus as their Savior.

50. _____ I am not afraid to challenge someone if I know it will foster spiritual growth and boldness in their life.

51. _____ I will boldly move forward in a situation if I sense God's calling and provision to do so.

52. _____ I believe I have been blessed financially so that I may be a blessing to the church and her mission to reach the lost and help the poor.

53. _____ I retain most of what I learn and can recall it quickly when the need arises.

54. _____ I can readily identify leaders and love to help them grow in their gifts and abilities.

55. _____ I love to see people through the storms of life and show them the compassion that Jesus did.

56. _____ I care about the church and do all I can to see it grow and be built up in love.

57. _____ God has put in my mind urgent matters that were otherwise unknown that I have announced to the church.

58. _____ I set aside time in my week to help those in need in my church and community.

59. _____ I hate it when someone uses Scripture out of context for their own purposes.

60. _____ I can see where a group or individual's decisions and actions will lead them, and I offer to guide them in the right direction.

61. _____ Details matter to me and I pay special attention to make sure things are done correctly.

62. _____ I am qualified and able to establish and lead a new church or ministry.

63. _____ I can often tell if someone is being deceitful or dishonest before it becomes apparent to others.

64. _____ I love to share what Christ has done in my life and how He has changed me.

65. _____ Others have told me that my words have compelled them to step out and grow in their faith.

66. _____ Even when times are tough, I trust God completely to comfort me and provide for my needs.

67. _____ Stewardship is an important discipline in my daily walk with Christ.

68. _____ I like to share the truth and insights God has shown me with others.

69. _____ People often look to me to lead a group or project.

70. _____ I have been known to "care too much" and help others in their time of need.

71. _____ I long to see each person in the church fulfilling the Great Commission.

72. _____ I have suddenly received a message from God specific to our congregation and shared it for the edification of the entire church.

73. _____ If I recognize a need in the church I simply fill it without being asked.

74. _____ I pay attention to the words people use because each one is significant and has meaning.

75. _____ It is humbling to me when someone asks for my guidance, so I take great care to help them.

76. _____ I manage my time wisely.

77. _____ I have a strong desire to raise up leaders and pastors who will equip the church.

78. _____ Things tend to be black or white to me; I see things as good or evil, right or wrong, true or false.

79. _____ I am not afraid to plead with people to believe that Christ died for their sin and to confess Him as Lord and Savior.

80. _____ When others are faced with difficult situations, I boldly tell them of the faithfulness of God towards His people.

81. _____ I don't often worry because of my confidence in God's ability and willingness to see me through every circumstance.

82. _____ I seek ways to help others financially and share the love of Christ with them.

83. _____ I am able to relate the truth and realities of the Gospel to all aspects of life.

84. _____ I am not afraid to step up and take charge in a crisis situation.

85. _____ I seek out those who are deemed "lost causes" and aid them in restoring their lives.

86. _____ The Gospel of Jesus Christ is the foundation of my life and ministry.

87. _____ Others have recognized that often God has spoken clearly and directly to them through a message I have shared.

88. _____ I believe there is eternal significance in performing mundane tasks and service.

89. _____ I love discovering how the Gospel is woven throughout the entire Bible as I increasingly spend time in study.

90. _____ I can easily see which plan or strategy is the best one in a given circumstance.

91. _____ My desk or workspace is set up so I can access whatever I need quickly.

92. _____ Other pastors and leaders often come to me for help and guidance.

93. _____ Others have told me that my perceptions or judgments of people, situations, or statements have proved trustworthy.

94. _____ Most of my conversations with non-Christians lead to me speaking about my faith in Jesus.

95. _____ If a person or a group is stumbling or deviating from the life God has intended for them, I will speak up and press them to remember and return to joyful life in Christ.

96. _____ I consistently encourage others to trust God in everything.

97. _____ I give generously and without pretense to the ministry of God's people.

98. _____ I can usually recall a Scripture verse or passage that applies to a given situation.

99. _____ I am more "visionary" than detail oriented. I concentrate more on the big picture than the day-to-day particulars.

100._____ Others have showed appreciation that I have comforted and ministered to them at a low point in their lives.

101. _____ I do not seek the "spotlight," but God has called me to shepherd His people.

102._____ I am always listening for the Spirit of God and I am open to receiving whatever message He has for me to share.

103._____ I find joy in being a helper and assisting others in their ministries.

104._____ Often the Holy Spirit gives me just the right words to say when I am teaching an individual or group.

105. _____ I can often see through the confusion or conflict in a situation and provide a practical and Scriptural solution to it.

Scoring Directions:

Write your score (from 0-5) for each question in the box with that question number. Add up each column and write your total scores above the corresponding Gift Code. Once you have done this you can check the key below to see what spiritual gift each Gift Code represents. The highest score for any gift is 35. The higher the score, the stronger you are in that spiritual gift based on your responses.

Scoring Matrix

1	2	3	4	5	6	7	8	9	10	11	12	13	14	15
16	17	18	19	20	21	22	23	24	25	26	27	28	29	30
31	32	33	34	35	36	37	38	39	40	41	42	43	44	45
46	47	48	49	50	51	52	53	54	55	56	57	58	59	60
61	62	63	64	65	66	67	68	69	70	71	72	73	74	75
76	77	78	79	80	81	82	83	84	85	86	87	88	89	90
91	92	93	94	95	96	97	98	99	100	101	102	103	104	105

	1	2	3	4	5	6	7	8	9	10	11	12	13	14
Total Scores														
Gift Codes	Ad	Di	Ev	EX	Fa	Gi	Kn	Le	Me	Pa	Pr	Se	Te	Wi

Gift Codes:

Ad = Administration **Ap** = Apostleship **Di** = Discernment **Ev** = Evangelism **Ex** = Exhortation **Fa** = Faith **Gi** = Giving **Kn** = Knowledge **Le** = Leadership **Me** = Mercy **Pa** = Pastor/Shepherd **Pr** = Prophecy **Se** = Serving/Ministering **Te** = Teaching **Wi** = Wisdom

The Conclusion

One day when you have time, please go through the Bible and you will find biblical instruction in which we are all called to live. However, we are called to train. Proverbs 22:6 states: "Train up a child in the way he should go; even when he is old he will not depart from it." Paul instructs Titus by saying "Likewise, urge the younger men to be self-controlled. Show yourself in all respects to be a model of good works, and in your teaching show integrity, dignity, and sound speech that cannot be condemned, so that an opponent may be put to shame, having nothing evil to say about us" (Titus 2:6-8). And we have found the great instruction he gave Timothy.

The idol or the object of the study was to put the Word of God in action in your life. To be intentional in demonstrating the love of God and fulling the Paul instructed Timothy to instill in the minds and hearts of the Christian in his day the truths they had heard and received from the Lord Jesus.

If you would allow the Holy Spirit to lead you through each section and faithful to His voice!

1. **Have you put your HOPE/FAITH in the living God?**

2. **Sinners Prayer:**
   Father God, I know that I have broken your laws and my sins have separated me from you.
   I am truly sorry. And now I want to turn away from my past sinful life, and turn toward you.
   Please forgive me, and help me avoid sinning again.
   I believe that your son Jesus Christ died for my sins, was resurrected from the dead, is alive and hears my prayer.
   I invite you Jesus to become the Lord of my life. To rule and reign in my heart from this day forward. Now please send your Holy Spirit to help me to obey You, and to do Your will for the rest of my life.
   In Jesus' name, I pray, Amen."

References

1. YOUTH SPIRITUAL GIFTS TEST and ADULT SPIRITUAL GIFTS TEST - Copyright © 2013-2015 www.SpiritualGiftsTest. com. All rights reserved.

"Your Religion Lived Out Loud" as you "Grow from Milk to Meat"

"PUTTING THE WORD OF GOD IN ACTION!"

Rev. Dr. Calvin L. McCullough Sr.

Graduate of Jacksonville Theological Seminary, Jacksonville, Florida; Master of Theology degree; May 2008 and a Doctorate of Ministry Degree; February 2011.

Graduate of Queen City Bible College, Charlotte, North Carolina; earned dual degrees; Bachelor of Biblical Studies and a Bachelor of Pastoral Studies; June 2007.

Graduate of Liberty University Home Bible Institute in Lynchburg, Virginia; 2003 a Diploma of Biblical Courses.

VISION STATEMENT:

It is my VISION is to see every Man, Woman, Boy and Girl come to know Jesus Christ as their Lord and Savior.

MISSION STATEMENT:

It is my MISSION to make known the biblical and historical person and works of Jesus Christ; with the purpose of persuading every person I come in contact with to put their trust in him exclusively, as their only means of salvation, to the glory of God.

PURPOSE STATEMENT:

As a Christian, I understand that I am a servant and stewards of the Lord Jesus Christ and have been entrusted with individual in my circle of influence. As a Christian I understand it's my responsibility to help develop them mentally, physically, and spiritually, to the glory of God.

PERSONAL STATEMENT:

"We must tell the people about the gospel of Jesus Christ!" There are many types of diseases all over the world: mental, physical, and spiritual, such as Aids, cancer, heart disease, also adultery, violence, lust, and pride. However, the ultimate disease of all time is SIN, which has been man's problem from the beginning of creation. We have been given the answer to their eternal problem and the answer is Jesus Christ. It is our duty to make the proclamation of the biblical and historical person and works of Jesus Christ known, with the purpose of persuading men and women all over the world to put their trust in Him exclusively as their only means of salvation. With this cure, people can rise above poverty, be freed from the bondage of sin, and their eyes and hearts may be open to the truth.

Motto: "There is nothing too hard for God!"
(Genesis 18:14; Job 42:2; Jeremiah 32:17, 27)

Printed in the United States
by Baker & Taylor Publisher Services